AWAY from the BALL

AWAY
from the BALL

THE NFL'S OFF-THE-FIELD HEROES

ALAN ROSS

CUMBERLAND HOUSE
NASHVILLE, TENNESSEE

Away from the Ball
Published by Cumberland House Publishing Inc.
431 Harding Industrial Drive
Nashville, TN 37211

Cover design: Gore Studio, Inc.
Text design: John Mitchell
Virtual assistants: Cindy McLaughlin, Joanne Cooper, Brandie Eads, Anna Lavigne

Library of Congress Cataloging-in-Publication Data
Ross, Alan.
  Away from the ball : The NFL's off-the-field heroes / Alan Ross.
    p. cm.
  Includes bibliographical references and index.
  ISBN-13: 978-1-58182-654-8 (hardcover : alk. paper)
  ISBN-10: 1-58182-654-0 (hardcover : alk. paper)
  1. National Football League—Biography. 2. Football players—United States—Conduct of life.
3. Football players—United States—Biography. I. Title.

GV955.5.N35R665 2008
796.3320922—dc22
[B]

                          2008016482

Printed in Canada

1 2 3 4 5 6 7—14 13 12 11 10 09 08

For
Ed "E" Kelley, my old Cranwell roomie,
who I doubt will recall that he unwittingly planted the
seed for this book in a phone conversation two years ago
and
sweet Caroline,
for her limitless love and inexhaustible help
in every area of my life; my backbone, my raison d'etre

CONTENTS

Lee Reeves, the author, George Martin

PREFACE

It would be nearly impossible to guess when philanthropy first hit sport's big stage. Altruism in athletics as recently as fifty years ago had little or no identity, no face, and scant visibility with the public. Doubtless, athletes were doing good deeds that benefited others. We just didn't hear about them. The only example that immediately comes to mind of an athlete gaining some renown for his compassionate acts was a superstar: Babe Ruth. And, if you think about it, we likely wouldn't have heard a peep about the Babe's visits to sick children in hospitals if he *hadn't* been a superstar. The National Football League, fortunately, has a somewhat clearer map of its legacy of philanthropy.

During World War II, the league helped sell war bonds and donated the revenue from fifteen preseason games to service charities. Those games brought in $680,384.07, reportedly the largest amount raised by an athletic organization for the war effort. A trio of Green Bay Packers stars—Curly Lambeau, Don Hutson, and Cecil Isbell—merited Treasury Department citations for selling

$2,100,000 in war bonds in a single night at a rally in Milwaukee. During World War II, the Korean War, and Vietnam, more than twelve hundred NFL players, coaches, and team owners put their careers on hold to serve in the military. The venerable USO has been entertaining members of the armed services since 1942, and since 1979, the Dallas Cowboys Cheerleaders, the league's undisputed champs, have made more than sixty appearances for the organization. But it is the years 1967 and 1973 that stand as benchmarks in the NFL timeline of altruism, as the league instituted two major humanitarian efforts.

Green Bay Packers Hall of Fame quarterback Bart Starr was the first recipient of the Byron "Whizzer" White Humanitarian Award, presented by the NFL Players Association annually since 1967 to the NFL player who best serves his team, community, and country in the spirit of Byron Raymond "Whizzer" White, the late Supreme Court Justice. Talk about the ultimate role model: White was a Rhodes Scholar, humanitarian, patriot, and public servant who also managed to squeeze in three years of play in the NFL after a sensational collegiate career as a consensus All-America tailback at Colorado and Heisman Trophy runner-up in 1937. Offered a fortune at the time—$15,000—White, the first-round draft pick of the Pittsburgh Pirates, forerunners of the Steelers, ceremoniously signed with the team's young owner, Art Rooney. White rewarded his boss in his one and only season in the Iron City by leading the NFL in rushing and making first team All-Pro. He then left for Oxford to fulfill his Rhodes Scholarship commitment.

When he returned to the States, White signed with Detroit, playing with the Lions in 1940 and '41, and was named All-Pro a second time in '40 when he again led the league in rushing. His later Supreme Court career is well documented. The NFLPA says of White, "His service to the nation . . . brings honor upon every man in professional football." A complete list of Byron "Whizzer" White Award winners can be found in the Appendix.

In 1973, the NFL made an unprecedented connection with the United Way. It's said that when the charitable organization approached Pete Rozelle, the savvy young NFL czar who catapulted a mostly benign league to the pinnacle of American sport during his tenure as commissioner, he jumped at the chance to donate television airtime to help promote United Way's causes. Such an arrangement enabled Rozelle to showcase his players doing good things in their communities, putting a face on a product normally hidden under helmets. The cooperative effort placed the NFL far above other professional sports in philanthropic visibility. Through the long, collaborative series of television public service announcements with the United Way that began in 1974, the league began to secure its position as the leader in sports altruism.

Today, more than eight hundred United Way/NFL spots have aired since the inaugural batch in 1974. And what an array that was! Incredible as it sounds, the NFL and United Way filmed sixty-three individual PSAs that year, featuring such football luminaries as Franco Harris for the YWCA, Billy Kilmer for cerebral palsy, Bob Griese for Big Brothers, Floyd Little for multiple sclerosis, and Roger Staubach for open-heart surgery. In between, hundreds of other gridiron stars have stepped in front of the camera for United Way. Frank Gifford, Gale Sayers, Vince Lombardi, Tony Dorsett, Walter Payton, Paul Warfield, Sonny Jurgensen, Joe Montana, Don Shula, Eric Dickerson, Jerry Rice, Troy Aikman, Dan Marino, John Elway, the Dallas Cowboys Cheerleaders, and even early league immortals Ernie Nevers and Jim Thorpe have all helped create the personality of the NFL through the United Way spots.

Bringing it closer to home, George Martin, the former New York Giants defensive end profiled in the opening section of this book, filmed a United Way spot for the Cerebral Palsy Center back in 1979 and was named the Byron "Whizzer" White Award winner in 1987. The PSA series began introducing the wives of players into spots alongside their husbands in 1992, creating an even stronger visual image through the power of the family unit.

One of the earliest NFL public service announcements had a profound effect on former two-time world heavyweight boxing champion George Foreman. In an interview for a national magazine earlier this year, Foreman told me that he vividly recalled a PSA for the Job Corps, President Lyndon Johnson's national vocational training program in 1964. The spot featured two of Foreman's boyhood idols—NFL superstars Jim Brown and Johnny Unitas. Why did Foreman remember the spot so well, even the year that it ran? Quite simply, it changed his life.

"If those fellas said something, I certainly would do it," said Foreman in *American Profile*. The future Olympic gold medalist wound up, at age sixteen, enrolling in a Job Corps training center, from where he was introduced to mentors that helped forge his phenomenal ring career. "That commercial literally rescued me from the gutter," he said.

Philanthropy even runs in the family, as evidenced by football's so-called first family—the Mannings. In a generational oddity, twenty-seven years before Peyton Manning appeared in a 2002 United Way spot, his father Archie, the great New Orleans Saints quarterback of the late 1960s and '70s, was the subject of a 1975 United Way PSA that provided important information to the needy on resources available in communities, from food banks and shelters to after-school programs and rehab services.

In 1970, the NFL inaugurated its prestigious Man of the Year award, the league's most distinctive award for excellence both on and off the field. Baltimore Colts quarterback Johnny Unitas was the initial winner, and subsequent honorees have included the lustrous likes of Walter Payton (1977), for whom the award would be renamed in 1999; Roger Staubach (1978); late Kansas City Chiefs linebacker Derrick Thomas (1993), who also garnered the Byron "Whizzer" White Award in 1995; Warrick Dunn (2004), who is profiled extensively within these pages; and Peyton Manning (2005), who also claimed the White award in the same year.

In one rare instance, a philanthropic award was returned. Former Green Bay/Atlanta safety Eugene Robinson was presented the 1999 Bart Starr Award for model character and community humanitarianism but was arrested for soliciting a prostitute the day before he was to participate in Super Bowl XXXIII as a starter in the Falcons' secondary. When you look at the list of Bart Starr Award winners, you will see Robinson's name mentioned as the recipient in '99 but with a notation that the award was returned following his arrest. The list (minus the notation) appears in full in the Appendix.

The incident was a harbinger of darker days to come for the NFL. Beginning in 2005, a rash of negative events began burning down the wholesome image the league had so carefully cultivated since the Pete Rozelle era. The transgressions read like a riot act:

- Chicago Bears defensive tackle Tank Johnson (later signed by Dallas) unflatteringly distinguishes himself with numerous run-ins with the law, including charges of aggravated assault and resisting arrest after threatening a police officer, all while on parole.
- Tennessee Titans cornerback Adam "Pacman" Jones owns a rap sheet longer than a commencement speech, including being named as the possible force behind the shooting of three people in a Las Vegas club in February 2007.
- Bears linebacker Lance Briggs totals his $350,000 Lamborghini on an expressway then bolts from the accident scene.
- New England Patriots head coach Bill Belichick okays sign-stealing measures against the New York Jets in a flagrant trampling of the game's rules of fair play.

But all that paled in comparison to the blockbuster news that Atlanta Falcons super quarterback Michael Vick had bankrolled a dog-fighting racket. For his unthinking indiscretions, Vick was sentenced to twenty-three months in federal prison and a possible, though unlikely, lifetime expulsion from the National Football League.

It didn't stop with the NFL either. Illicit drug use and gambling continue to capture the headlines in other sports: referees on the take in the NBA; few clean competitors in the sports of cycling and track and field; baseball's Barry "Balco" Bonds and seven-time Cy Young Award winner Roger Clemens giving up their names to disgrace.

The good guys seem conspicuously absent, eclipsed by the higher decibel level of sensationalism.

For the most part, the media has an abiding love affair with negativity and muckraking—yellow journalism, they call it. That means the public rarely hears the good-news opposite of the bad news conveyed. We don't hear enough about people like Indianapolis Colts head coach Tony Dungy, whose humanistic approach to coaching athletes flies in the face of the traditional drill-sergeant-molded NFL. And there's Tampa Bay Buccaneers running back Warrick Dunn, whose selfless giving in the Tampa, Atlanta, Baton Rouge, and Tallahassee communities helps single mothers into their first homes, by supplying down-payment assistance and complete home furnishings. Both men have rebounded from personal tragedy to tirelessly work to improve the lives of others.

Imagine former New York Giants defensive end George Martin —at age fifty-five—walking across America to raise funds for the families of 9/11 first responders! The lives of these NFL men reflect the respect earned from their caring acts. To them, it has never been about obtaining recognition, but the well-being of people in need.

While the closing chapter singles out twenty current or former NFL players who are making significant differences today through their charitable and humanitarian efforts, the book's purpose is to go beyond the dollar amounts generated, the routine listing of community and civic credits, and the glittering awards often presented at black-tie affairs. Though it would have been great to cite the vast number of generous-hearted humanitarians throughout the league, the intent was to explore in depth a more manageable number. I'm pleased to present three outstanding philanthropists involved with the NFL today: a current player, a coach, and a player alumnus. Hopefully, it is an honest look at their impeccable character.

—A. R.

ACKNOWLEDGMENTS

Many people were exceedingly generous in so many different ways with their time and assistance in helping me put together this look at philanthropy in the NFL. Thank you all *so* much. Especially:

Cindy McLaughlin, Brandie Eads, Anna Lavigne, and Joanne Cooper, you are my champions, transcriptionists from heaven!

A major thanks to Lee Reeves, general manager and chief technical advisor for George Martin's "A Journey for 9/11" walk; Natalie Boe, executive director of the Warrick Dunn Foundation; and All Pro Dad Public Relations Director Darrin Gray for their inestimable help in putting together the chapters on George Martin, Warrick Dunn, and Tony Dungy.

Thanks also to Anna Isaacson, National Football League manager of community affairs; Allison Stangeby, New York Giants community relations director; Joanna Comfort, NFL Players Association communications assistant; Tracey Holmes, director, NFL Partnership for United Way of America; and Indianapolis Colts Vice President of Public Relations Craig Kelley for their helpful assistance and prompt replies to requests along the way.

My deepest thanks to George Martin, Lee Reeves, Dianne Martin, George Diaz, Daren Taylor, Patra Minocha, Tony Dungy, Jeff Saturday, Abe Brown, Darrin Gray, Pat Fitzgerald, Steve Blaising, Warrick Dunn, Natalie Boe, Melanie Keith, Otis Keith, Rita Arena, Tiffany Miles, Billy Miles, Beth Stubbings, Rona Nasiri, Jacquelyn Williams, Joele Fanning, Kia Savage, Shannon Sanders, and Jennifer Krix for their forthright interviews and generous time in rendering such. Without them, this book doesn't get made.

Enduring gratitude and most sincere appreciation to my long-time editor and dear friend John Mitchell, and a special thanks to all at Cumberland House.

AWAY from the BALL

PART ONE

GEORGE MARTIN
The Transcontinental Traverse

Chapter One

"LET ME BE THE ONE"

The walker's pace is steady and determined. Just west of Cookeville, Tennessee, former New York Giants defensive end George Martin is striding along the shoulder of U.S. 70 on a clear and unseasonably mild November day. In his spandex out-doorwear and Giants-issue pullover, Martin is a physical specimen, his massive six-foot-four, 245-pound frame giving onlookers the unmistakable impression of mayhem once rendered on the field of play. Twenty years after his last game with New York, he still looks like he could take the field today, and give Giant defensive ends Osi Umenyiora and Michael Strahan a run for their money.

Martin is on an improbable journey for a man of fifty-five, one that even a conditioned athlete would find daunting. He's walking across America to raise money to benefit seriously ill Ground Zero rescue and recovery workers, the "first responders" during the infamous 9/11 attack, who were exposed to life-threatening toxins, the later effects of which are now coming to the surface. The walk kicked off at the George Washington Bridge on September 16, 2007, and ambled south through New Jersey, Pennsylvania, Delaware, Maryland, and Washington D.C., before moving into the sweeping hills and pastoral countryside of Virginia, and now Tennessee, the seventh state traversed.

One naturally wonders about the personal impetus behind such an undertaking. Countless ways exist in which noble efforts can be aided or an awareness raised about a worthy cause, but walking the length of the country?

"That's always been the proverbial question," says Martin, as we pace west along the rural Tennessee terrain. "It's a blending of two distinct passions that I have. First and foremost, as a country boy, I've always had the wanderlust of seeing what was on the other side of the ridge or just around the bend. I've always wanted to explore America, and I've done it in a car. I've driven across America three times, and I think the ultimate way to do it is to do it on foot. I've always been predisposed to doing this, but I decided if I were going to do something of this magnitude, why not connect a cause associated with it? To me, there was no better cause than the Journey for 9/11. I love it, and that just seemed a natural."

A transplanted thirty-year New Yorker—he was born in South Carolina—Martin witnessed the shattering events of 9/11 up close and personal, losing two people in the terrorist attack that he knew: twenty-three-year-old New Jersey neighbors Christian DeSimone and Tyler Ugolyn.

"It happened right in my backyard," he says soberly. "The thing that always struck me was how these brave men and women rushed into this imminent danger zone, and they did it without regard to their careers, their health, their safety. In retrospect, they were responding to the darkest day in American history. As I followed it, I found out they had subjected themselves to some health issues, and we were not responding in kind as a nation. Now the families of those heroes are on welfare."

Around the time Martin and the crew for A Journey for 9/11 were passing through central Virginia in the fall of 2007, the *New York Times* was running articles detailing woes befalling first responders, including some who were experiencing pulmonary fibrosis from inhaling excessive ash at Ground Zero. That condition causes scar tissue to build up on the lungs that could lead to transplants. As recently as February 2008, HBO ran a documentary rife with the myriad health problems affecting first responders.

"It's always easy to point an accusing finger at someone else," says Martin, "so I just decided not to be a detractor and to go out and say, 'You know what? If something is gonna make a difference, let me be the one to make that difference. And that's how our project was born.'"

Martin has spoken with countless individuals directly affected by the terror attacks of 9/11 and relates the wealth of humanity found in each encounter. "They're all heart-wrenching; they're all just so

COURTESY OF A JOURNEY FOR 9/11

Martin huddles with George Diaz and Lee Reeves (right) at the Virginia-Tennessee border.

emotionally entwined," he says. "Each person that you talk to, they come up to you and embrace you; you're a total stranger, and they have this look of such appreciation. It just tells you that you're doing the right thing and you're doing it for the right reason. It's going to help the right cause.

"I've had so many of those experiences; there are almost too many to recount right now. That's what makes it so deeply personal, and that's why never a moment during this eight hundred miles so far have I ever had a second thought or any regrets whatsoever. That's really the crux of the matter; that's what it's really all about."

A long way from Guttenberg

Two days before Thanksgiving, I meet the Journey for 9/11 team in the lobby of the Country Inns & Suites in Cookeville, Tennessee, their home base for several days, as Martin logs miles west of the city. They will camp near Nashville after tomorrow's walk. Dianne, Martin's wife of thirty-five years, is hoping they can find a soup kitchen or some place to volunteer their efforts on that special day of thanks.

It is lunchtime as Martin, who has already walked his morning miles, rests in his room before the afternoon session of pounding more pavement. Accompanying him on the expedition is a no-frills staff that includes Dianne, serving as event coordinator, and Lee Reeves, Martin's trusted friend and the Journey team's general manager and chief technical advisor. George Diaz fills a dual capacity as the party's EMT and SUV driver, patrolling the road ahead of and behind Martin for potential hazards that might suddenly loom. Daren Taylor is also on board for security detail from Beau Dietl and Associates, a three-week rotational position that is generally filled by retired New York Police Department or Fire Department officers.

Martin joins us after his rest period, and soon I'm following the crew out to the point along U.S. 70 where Martin left off that morning. The beginning/ending point each day is scrupulously determined by the satellite GPS unit aboard the official Journey for 9/11 vehicle, a white Chevy Trail Blazer, the back and sides of which are emblazoned with "George" and "Martin" on either side of the license plate and the project's Web address below the plate: www.ajourneyfor911.info. Bumper stickers for NYPD and FDNY shout "Never Forget." A simple strategy helps the Martin entourage plan its nightly accommodations: the troupe stays at a motel a few miles beyond or behind the next sizeable community along the route, and Diaz then shuttles Martin and Reeves to and from the exact starting or finishing point, based on the GPS readout.

"What we found out works best for us is to just move once a week," Dianne says. "We were moving every couple of days, and that drags on you after a while. So we move once a week. We've been here in Cookeville since they started walking from Knoxville to here. So they walked towards Cookeville, now they're a little past it. That has worked out better for us. That way, we do have time, if someone is sending something to us, to know ahead of time what hotel we'll be at so that it doesn't miss us."

As the Martins have discovered during the course of their journey, a solid plan like the one outlined above comes in mighty handy. As fall 2007 segued into winter, hurried calls were placed back to the New York Giants offices—an S.O.S. of sorts, really—to have Giants cold-weather gear expressed to Martin ASAP.

"Allison Stangeby of the New York Giants community relations department was able to hook us up with Joe Browne at the National Football League office, and they connected us with a company that sent out three big boxes of coats and gloves, long pants, and waterproof gear," recounts Martin's wife. "Nike is one of our sponsors, and they've been very good to us. They sent mostly jogging pants and stuff that you'll see on him today. Not heavy-duty stuff. I think they weren't thinking that we would be walking in this kind of weather. If you're not thinking forward," she says of connecting with planned package deliveries, "you don't pick it up."

Not fifteen minutes from the hotel, we have arrived at Martin's starting point. He and Reeves debark, as I'm instructed to continue up the road several miles and find an appropriate place to park my car. George Diaz follows in the official Journey SUV and will shuttle me back to rejoin them. On the trip back, I wonder out loud to Diaz how he got involved as the Martin mission's EMT and driver.

"My friend, who owns an ambulance company, knows the treasurer of the board for Journey for 9/11," says Diaz, "He asked if I knew anyone who wanted to go out on a pretty long road trip. I asked around—mostly friends I knew who worked for other transport companies in emergency services—but none could do it. They all had families or other jobs. So, I said, 'I'll do it. I'll help you out.' Then I went to see Mrs. Martin. From there we hit it off, and I've been with them since the beginning."

Of the many things Diaz had experienced up to that point on the trek, he rates the day-to-day process of people stopping the team to donate money and to ask questions about the cause as truly memorable. "It's a great thing. You don't see this around where we live," says the twenty-four-year-old Diaz, from Guttenberg, New Jersey. "No one's going to pull over to ask you questions. People are just going to ignore you in passing traffic. But here, everybody's greeted us with open hearts and open arms. Ever since we stepped into the state of Tennessee, everyone's been just so great to us. It's a beautiful thing that people would want to sit down with you and converse about the whole journey."

Diaz, whose services are paid for not by Martin but by Kevin Fuchs, Diaz's employer and the owner of Fuchs E.M.S. and Medical Transport Services in Fair Lawn, New Jersey, says that Virginia originally set the level for hospitality on the walk. "But once we crossed over, I think Tennessee has been the best." The trip is a guaranteed eye-opener for Diaz, who had never been farther west of the New York metropolitan area than Pennsylvania. "It's been the best. I love it."

East-West meets North-South

Diaz's cell phone beeps as we ride. Lee Reeves is on the other end, urging us to rejoin them quickly. Apparently they've run into some interesting folks. Several minutes later, we're standing at the corner of Hewitt Ridge Road and U.S. 70 with John and Dave Messick, a father and son making an extended bicycling trip.

The two were heading eastbound on Highway 70 when they encountered the Journey for 9/11 crew. "They saw us on this side of the road and decided, 'Okay, we're going to come over and check this out,'" Lee says of their meeting. Son John had begun his journey from a little town in northwest Wisconsin called Rice Lake. Two weeks later, dad Dave, also a Wisconsin resident, hooked up with his son in Columbia, Missouri, where John had attended the University of Missouri, and from there they lit out together.

"We're headed east, toward North Carolina," the younger Messick indicates. "We're going to [follow] the coast down to Miami. We're not sure what route we're going to take yet."

"I'm just following him," says Dave Messick. "He's finding America and I'm following him. If you want to spend time with your kid, you gotta get on a bicycle."

John says his intent when setting off on the trek was "to see if people are as inhospitable as the rest of the world thinks."

Many people I know feel the way John did before he embarked on his North-South quest. Doubt and uneasiness have poured consistently from a growing mistrust and disillusionment with our country's leaders, spawning fear and suspicion among people everywhere. Fortunately, the younger Messick, on his defining journey, is being shown otherwise.

"So far I've debunked that myth completely," he says. "It's been fantastic. I've had nothing but great experiences."

In their travels, John and his father have discovered some inter-esting differences about large and small towns. "I find it's harder to talk to people along the highways when you get to these big high-way towns," John says. "When you're going out of town, you got your Applebee's and your giant Wal-Mart, and you've got these strip malls that go two or three miles out of town. We can't really find too many people. When you stay in a hotel, you can't really go anywhere 'cause you're on foot. So, it's interesting that the smaller the town, the easier it is to get around. The downtowns in the big-ger towns are always dead. There's nothing to do; you have to go out on the highway to do it."

Unlike the Journey team, the Messicks were facing a time dead-line. "We've got tickets out of Miami on Christmas Eve," notes John. "We're flying home."

Lee leads some humorous banter with the Messicks and suggests pictures be taken all around. An informal discussion of the dates for the pair's return to Wisconsin elicits laughter from Reeves, as he prods Martin good-naturedly about A Journey for 9/11's own itin-erary—a topic about which all concerned have differing opinions. Projecting exact dates and times when the Journey team will be traveling through a certain area is difficult, and, because of George's celebrity and such unplanned functions as visiting firehouses, it is even more problematic to schedule local media coverage very far in advance. Delays are, simply, inevitable.

"That's why I carry the big stick," says Lee, laughing. "Every time we start talking dates, I need protection from George."

The comment is amusing because Martin always lowballs a proj-ected arrival date. If Dianne and Lee calculate they will be in a particu-lar city by mid-February, George may disagree and submit an earlier date, thinking he can pick up the pace if they've had a delay. This sparks an ongoing debate/argument. Lee's mention of the "big stick" is a reference to the pole he carries while walking alongside or slightly ahead of Martin to fend off anything untoward they may encounter.

"This is deterrence in the event we run into an aggressive dog or an aggressive individual," says Reeves about the stick, adding that Martin never carries it. "We don't want him to seem aggressive by carrying one. He's a big enough guy as it is."

Both parties extend heartfelt goodbyes and a round of good luck.

The 40 Bridge

Dianne Martin's role as event coordinator calls for her to stay back at the motel and work to alert media in upcoming towns of the Journey team's impending arrival. You won't see the Martin caravan camping out along the side of the road anywhere, but General Electric, a tour sponsor, has provided a custom motor coach—replete with a Fathead-size likeness of Martin in his old No. 75 Giants uniform on the rear side panels—for those l-o-o-o-n-n-g desolate stretches of the Texas-Oklahoma panhandle and the southwestern states of New Mexico and Arizona where nearly anything that appears to be a motel is a mirage.

The Trail Blazer's GPS system is a vital player in Martin's effort. He is insistent that literally every foot of every mile between New York and San Francisco be walked, so establishing the exact beginning and ending point of each day's walk is crucial. Only once during the Journey—from New York City through Cookeville, where we were—had Martin been foiled, and that was for just a brief span near Perryville, Maryland. It was simply unavoidable.

"The only impasse that we had was when we got to a bridge in Maryland called the 40 Bridge," recalls Reeves. "We couldn't walk across that bridge. I tried everything. The day we were approaching the bridge, I noticed they were doing construction and had a lane shut down. So I tried to get them to allow us to walk in that lane that was shut down. The answer was no.

"But a Corporal LeBrun—I'll never forget him; he could not have been more accommodating—was trying to help us solve this

General Electric provided this custom motor coach for Martin's "A Journey for 9/11" cross-country walk, a welcome haven for the team in desolate areas where anything resembling a motel is a mirage.

problem of getting George from Point A to Point B," he continues. "He was with the Maryland Transportation Authority. He told me, 'You know, if you go down this street and go down that way and go across, there's a dam.' And he says you can't really cross that bridge where the dam is either, but it's a 'don't ask, don't tell.' He says, 'If you try to cross the 40 Bridge, there are toll booths there. The second they see you, they're going to call us.' And he says even if I drag my feet, 'I'm still going to get you before you can get across that bridge.' He says, 'I don't care how far, or how fast he walks, there's no way he's going to get across that bridge. The only way you're going to get across that bridge is if the governor calls me and tells me.'

"So now I've got to go to George and deliver that news to him," Reeves continues. "And when I talk to George about it, he says, 'The objective of this is not to ruffle anyone's feathers. The objective is to raise the consciousness of America about the problem and to raise the funds for these guys. So if you're telling me you've exhausted all resources except the governor and I can't get across that bridge, then it's not a big deal.' He said, 'The big deal is the education. I don't want any negative publicity or attention associated with this.'

"So I went and had another conversation with Corporal LeBrun, and he says, 'Not a problem.' He says, 'I'm going to have my guys meet you on this side of the bridge.' He says, 'I'm going to get it on videotape; I'm going to let them know what the problem was.' He says, 'I'll take you across the bridge in our cruisers, and when I get to the other side of the bridge, I'll document and verify the length of the bridge and why you had to get in a car.' He couldn't have been more accommodating. We ended up having lunch at the firehouse in that community. We had this barbecue again."

Dianne and Lee both laugh: more pig. It is a humorous running commentary among the team. "We were pigged out," recalls Reeves, of the almost nonstop diet of pork and barbecue everyone had ingested throughout the journey. "Everywhere we'd go, there was a pig place—pork this, pork this, pork that," he says, shaking his head.

"The fire department was there, the police department came over, and we broke bread," says Reeves, continuing the story. "We had a wonderful time. George had a brief nap by the park, and they took us across the bridge in the cruisers. My fiancée and I were in our car filming this as they took us across the bridge, so we could document that this is the only stretch that he didn't walk. It was one point two miles. Of the entire journey so far, that one-point-two miles is the only length that he could not walk."

A person conceivably could be excused for thinking that some slight fudging on such a lengthy undertaking as a walk across the country might be acceptable. Not Martin.

"He wants to walk the whole thing," reiterates Dianne, "and he keeps saying, 'I'm *going* to walk the whole thing.'"

Reeves reemphasizes the point. "In the beginning, I said, 'George, maybe we can alternate. Maybe I can walk five and let you take a rest.' He says, 'Yeah, you can walk the five, but I'm still going to walk the five, too.' We have Beau Dietl here to validate it, because at the end of this trip we need somebody to certify that he's walked every step. If he stops at this point at the end of the day, he can't start right here," says Reeves, moving his finger slightly forward on the GPS screen inside the car. "He has to come back to the stopping point, and that becomes his starting point for the next day."

The exact location is tracked several ways. After marking the stopping point at the close of each day in the GPS system, the information is then communicated to a young staffer, Jennifer Skor, the project's chief technical architect and mapping SME (Subject Matter Expert) in Connecticut. She's better known among the crew as "the Wizard Behind the Curtain" who monitors, tracks, and logs all data for the team.

"The first thing she said to us when we talked to her about doing this was, 'As long as you guys can walk and work around my mommy hours, then I'm okay,'" Reeves recollects. "That's the best investment we've made so far."

Chapter Two

THE MISSION FACE

A Journey for 9/11 is a no-nonsense walking venture from Martin's standpoint. He has a couple of different gears, and his extreme patience is severely tested when a less-than-steady walking pace generated by neophytes, well-intending well-wishers, and journalists results in fewer miles covered that day. George Martin's pace is not your pace or my pace. At his best, he will attack the road at more than a five-mile-per-hour clip. The man is flat hoofin' it. "Oh, he's hoofin' it, all right," acknowledges Dianne, delivering the line with just the right mixture of comedy and awe.

Reeves echoes Dianne's sentiments about George's grinding pace. "The most impressive thing about George is, he's on a mission," says Reeves, forty-nine, who first met Martin back in 1989 when both were working for Mutual of New York financial services. "He's got to get from Point A to Point B. Dianne will tell you that the biggest fights we have are about how long it's going to take to get from Point A to Point B. If you see this man walk, you'll know he's on a mission. If I happen to be in the car, I have a tendency to

watch the speedometer, and you see that needle is hovering at about
five miles per hour or above. So he's on a mission."

Reeves, it is clear, has made a study of Martin's remarkable pace
from his unique vantage point. "He does not slow down for the
mountains," notes Reeves. "Same pace on the flats, same pace on
the mountains. But let someone pull over and stop and ask a question about the Journey, and he will tell me to get out and have a
conversation with them if I'm in the car. If I'm walking with him,
he'll tell me to have a conversation with them. He does not leave
until they leave. He stops and he talks. But again, this is a man,
when he starts walking, he's on that mission. Nothing can stop him.
He figures if they can take the time out of the day to honk a horn,
wish him well, say hello, or make a donation, then he's also going to
take the time."

Martin's accelerated pace soon has me dropping back with
Reeves, the distance quickly widening between the front-walking
former Giant and the two of us. With a knowing nod and a hushed
tone of respect, Reeves rhapsodizes on the many facets of George
Martin. "The face that you're seeing," he nods ahead to his fast-dis-
appearing friend, "that's not his angry face. He's got an angry face."

When asked what face Martin currently has on, the trip's chief
technical advisor advises, "That's the mission face. Then he's got
the angry face."

The angry face. One imagines the massive Martin splitting
through the seams of his outer activewear, a large red and blue S on
the front of his shirt, scowl curling his lower lip, rage burning just
below boiling, forging a pace like a rabbit at a dog track, sneering at
trucks, autos, motorcycles, and any other vehicle attempting to
maintain his manic pace.

"The angry face is 'get your roller skates,'" Reeves says in a no-
foolin' tone. "Hop on something motorized to keep up with him."

One can immediately sense the inherent advantages in being six
feet four ("a forty-eight-inch thigh!" exclaims Reeves) that would

translate into a long stride. But professional athletes have another, more valuable resource: the ability to push past physical and mental barriers, a skill they have demonstrated on the field countless times under pressure throughout their careers. That difference quickly separates men from children on an endeavor like this one.

"He did thirty miles yesterday at this pace," says Reeves. "We're a little over three right now. So imagine thirty—ten times that—at this pace. You said you live two hours from here. How many miles is that?"

"Roughly a hundred twenty-five miles," I answer.

"Can you imagine walking that?"

"Frankly, no way," I say.

"Multiply that by six, and that's what George has walked so far." Reeves says, completing the illustration.

It is dumbfounding. Something on a cellular level must have registered inside me the afternoon before I went to meet with Martin. Anticipating a somewhat lengthy walk while interviewing him, I prepared by walking a half-mile in each of two different pairs of running shoes. I run regularly, but I own a pair of flat feet—not beneficial on a long walk. Finally, I wound up selecting the left shoe from one pair and the right shoe from the other set. I had related the shoe story to Dianne and Lee, telling them I couldn't believe the difference between walking and running. When you run, your feet hit the ground and are off again. But when walking, the feet absorb a different, more concentrated kind of stress. While I figured the offbeat appearance of my two-tone shoes would elicit hoots from the Journey assembly, it definitely offered my best shot at keeping up, albeit briefly, with the "mission" face of Martin. What I hadn't expected was total empathy and complete understanding on everyone's part.

"You'd be surprised how we're rotating shoes in and out," says Reeves. "The terrain is unpredictable out there." A chief concern for the Journey team is that the roads on the route often have little or no shoulder. "It can be very, very treacherous. In some instances it's a gravel falloff. We're constantly looking for places in case we have to ditch, but sometimes there's nowhere to ditch."

Reeves then recounts his physical travails along the way. "I had blisters on my feet, I lost two toenails. I got a third one coming off right now," he says of his podiatric ills. "Me, I'm not the professional athlete. I have a bandage holding one toenail on because I'm trying to get that undergrowth, that skin to toughen up. But if you think about what the first responders to 9/11 did, all of a sudden the toenail, the soreness, the aches and pains mean nothing."

Martin isn't one to suffer the petty physical annoyances of others. He and Reeves keep up a constant good-natured banter about challenges met and who scored what. The previous day, the final mileage tally came up different for Reeves than what Martin had logged for him. There was no disputing that Martin had put in thirty miles. It was Reeves's output that was under official review.

"He and I are fighting over that," Reeves chuckles. "I say I got twenty-six. He said I got twenty-five. As long as I keep the records, I got twenty-six." It appears the savvy Martin knows just when to praise and when to tase. "He came and acknowledged it [that Reeves had walked the twenty-five or twenty-six miles), which always makes me feel good. It's a tribute to his leadership, not to my fortitude. This is not a guy who hands out compliments."

The mile-after-mile pounding of the pavement wears down the feeble and the unfit. Not that Reeves isn't now in great shape himself after all the miles he has logged with Martin.

"I got up this morning thinking, *I'm not going to walk. I can't get a mile in,*" he says. "Then I listen to George's pep talk and we got out there. All of a sudden you forget you did a thirty-mile day yesterday.

Reeves has had his own trials matching Martin's grueling pace. On one particularly mountainous stretch of the Cumberland Plateau running vertically down through central-east Tennessee, Reeves feels he finally earned his stripes.

"We literally climbed a mountain that was two point two miles straight up," he remembers. "And I kept up with him every single step for step, at his pace, at that pace there," he says, pointing way up the road to Martin, striding along with his mission face on, "up that mountain for two point two miles. I think that's the day I earned his respect."

It conjures a time when people had to get everywhere by foot. Martin and Reeves would be the first to appreciate the toughness in that stock of earlier Americans. Dianne contributes a sobering comment that she had recently made to her husband:

"Nobody walks anymore."

A body for science

Martin more or less trivializes his own ailments, the result of focused hardening achieved over fourteen seasons of pro football warfare. In truth, he considers the shape his body is in today to be miraculous, considering the ordeals he endured on the gridiron.

"I'm thinking about willing my body to science when I'm done," Martin laughs. "Most people couldn't believe that anybody would be embarking on a journey like this, let alone a fourteen-year NFL defensive lineman. I went through fourteen years in the league and never had any surgery. On being discharged from the NFL, when I got my physical, the doctor looked at me and said, 'You sure you played in the NFL for fourteen years?' because all I had was a little crooked pinky finger. So here it is again, history repeating itself, the first eight hundred miles: no blisters, no pulled muscles, no strains, aches, and pains. It's unbelievable."

One is reminded of the exceedingly fortunate careers of two of the greatest running backs ever to play in the NFL—Jim Brown and Walter Payton. Both were able to leave the game without serious injury, an extraordinary rarity for the position they played. For a defensive lineman, the attainment of an injury-free career is no less amazing, almost unfathomable.

"It's really appropriate now," adds Martin, "with all the talk about the problems the older players are having with their benefits from the NFL. There are so many injury-prone careers, plus the lagging effects of having played in the NFL. I guess I'm the antithesis of that, 'cause I can't make any such claims. I feel great! I'm walking twenty-five, thirty miles a day. My knees are perfect, no swelling, no pain. Nothing in my hips, thighs, elbows, joints. To me, it's been remarkable."

Martin's enjoyment of excellent health these days may be attributable in part to a promise he once made with a former New York Giants teammate and Hall of Famer (2006), Harry Carson. The close friends made a pact between them that they would not become soft and out of shape in retirement. Twenty years after their final games as Giants in 1988, Carson and Martin have kept their promise.

"You know what? I think it's just fear," says Martin about his dedication to staying in shape and his pact with Carson, "because you realize you've already subjected yourself to an abbreviated lifespan by playing in the NFL, just from the rigors of it. Why go and jeopardize it further by exposing yourself to a sedentary lifestyle? I'll just put it that way."

The to and fro about athletes and injuries summons a time capsule from the early 1990s. I was at the Georgia Dome for a game at which the Atlanta Falcons introduced members of their early teams from the 1960s and '70s. I remember the great punter Billy Lothridge was introduced, and I think Tommy Nobis came out. In all, some forty players were introduced, brought out at halftime to midfield. The parade to the 50-yard line was a visual stunner: a *Dia de los Muertos* procession, the Bataan death march reincarnate. With the exception of perhaps two players, these old birds of prey needed to be helped onto the field, whether by a wheelchair, a cane, or an able-bodied caregiver.

I was agog at the toll. Here were these supermen of yesterday, now a feeble assembly of mere mortals, creaking shadows of their former selves and onetime greatness. That moving display of human deterioration made an indelible imprint on my comprehension of the game. The lasting physical effects are the least-discussed elements of a football player's life cycle with the sport. It is from this debilitative state that much of the players' bitterness toward the game and its current stewards is directed. One marvels again at Martin's fourteen-year NFL tenure without major injury.

"I've seen those images play out in my mind over the length of my career and beyond," says Martin, "and as former president of the NFL Players Association [Martin was the Giants' player representative for a decade and served as president of the NFLPA from 1987 to 1988, during a prickly period between labor and management], that was one of the big concerns: health benefits, medical benefits, pension benefits. I had seen so many of my predecessors [face health challenges]; it seemed the lot we were unfortunately destined for. How can we personally, individually, offset that? I mean, nutrition? Regular physicals? Prostate screening? All of the above?

"If you play this game for so long, for fourteen years, with some homicidal maniac yelling at you all the time, you would think that you would have the intestinal fortitude to say, 'You know, I'd like to be able to play with my kids or my grandkids, so keep the weight down, keep those good habits that you formed as a professional when you're no longer in that environment.' And that's what I've tried to do."

Not only is Martin doing it, he's inspiring those around him to do the same thing. I suggest to Lee Reeves that Martin's actions sound like those of a true leader.

"Oh he really is," agrees Reeves. "I don't have the reserve in my tank that he has. So he has to be the motivation for it."

Minor ailments aside, Martin may do his best motivating when inclement weather looms. "Not only does George have to do this [the walk], but he's got to motivate us on those days when it's rainy," says Reeves, "when your first inclination is to say, 'Ehhhhh, it's raining, it's cold outside, we're going to stay in.' Then you get the call from him: 'It's six o'clock.' And I'm telling you, that day I started out with the doom and gloom, George said something to us when we were in the car that really stuck. He said, 'We are going to be uncomfortable today, but think about what those firefighters and policemen did and the sacrifices they made,' which really put it into perspective."

Reeves worked in New York City and was there on 9/11. "We never felt like we did enough," he reflects. "And George's speech to us, well, all of a sudden, being out in the rain for a few minutes was nothing compared to those people that ran into a building knowing inevitably that there was a possibility of those buildings coming down."

Only the day before, the weather had yielded an odd photo-op situation that Reeves giggles at in recollection. "Imagine you're in the comfort of your car; you've got heat, you've got windshield wipers," Reeves begins. "We've walked in rainstorms, but yesterday the fog was so thick I had George Diaz taking pictures, and we couldn't see more than maybe ten or fifteen feet in front of us. It was like a cloud, like a drape around us. I told George, 'Get the camera; we've got to get some photos of this!' The media absolutely love those kinds of shots. It was really spectacular. When you're driving across the country, you don't get that. You don't get the flavor of the elements in the environment. The extreme heat, the extreme cold, the rain."

The remembrance conjures another, earlier rain memory for Reeves. "The first time we were out in a rainstorm, we were like kids," he says. "Big George is in the car, and he always says, 'First rule, safety first.' We pull up and it's raining outside and the traffic is heavy, and the first thing he says to his team is, 'Nobody is required to get out of this car but me. I'm going to get out; you guys just watch my back.' And immediately we all said, 'If you're getting out, we're getting out.'

Frigid temperatures provide extra motivation for Lee Reeves and George to keep hoofin' it.

"So we all got out. It was raining, it was cold, it was a miserable day to be outside. We couldn't have been more stupid. I mean, we were kids, little boys; we were even fighting in the rain. There was one, I got to tell you: I got this shot, and it made the cover of the *New York Post*. But I'm thinking, *I've got to get some shots of this rain,* because everybody keeps saying, the bad weather shots, those are the money shots.

"So I see this eighteen-wheeler coming, and I'm like, 'George, right there; just let me get the camera ready.' I'm looking around, and I can see this thing coming. I could see the mist coming off the back of this truck. I'm like, 'Okay, hold that pose.' I know I'm going to get soaked, too, but at least I'm going to get George in this shot. Just as the truck passes, I snap the picture. You can see him, just drenched with the water as the truck's coming by. I make the mistake of showing it to my fiancée. It was her camera I was using, so she didn't think it was very funny. I'm cracking up. This is funny!"

Reeves goes on to say that "a million stories" lie within the team's journey. "We've had stalkers, we've had magicians performing magic tricks on the side of the road, a city councilman massaging his feet," he says, still amazed. "A city councilperson taking George's shoes off, massaging his feet!" Turns out the official was a physical therapist on the side.

Accommodating councilpeople and bad-weather heroics notwithstanding, the troupe will actually postpone its agenda if extremely violent weather is forecast for an extended period. Dianne Martin recalls that the walk was temporarily scuttled while thunderstorms raged for days.

"We were in Virginia, and I think actually we had gone home," she says of the week's delay in Lynchburg in mid- to late October. "There were thunderstorms predicted for where we were going to be walking, so we just stayed home a few more days until the storms passed through. But George will walk in the rain. That doesn't bother him. And the other day, it snowed in the mountains in Tennessee, and they walked in that. It was cold, but that doesn't bother him either."

In-the-middle-of-nowhere man

In 1963, famed advertising guru David Ogilvy, in addition to heading up his top-performing Ogilvy & Mather international advertising agency, also managed to pen a No. 1 best-selling book, *Confessions of an Advertising Man*. In that landmark tome, Ogilvy talks about the mysteries of creation, about how we best place ourselves in a receptive mode for creative possibilities when "the mind lays fallow," as he put it. Lying fallow would include such mechanized but otherwise mindless endeavors as walking or jogging, and some would go so far as to include driving a car. Our motor is humming along, but our mind is in neutral. They say it yields powerful results.

With that in mind, I was curious to know if George ever let his mind loose on those long desolate stretches in the middle of nowhere, when traffic was at a minimum, during those rare times when he could walk uninterrupted for a while.

George laughs. "Boy, now you're really getting to the crux of the matter," he says. "I've always been a guy who never looked in the rearview mirror of his life. Never have. I've always looked ahead, and I can guarantee you that I'm looking at the next phase, the next chapter of my life—with my wife, hopefully, our grandchildren and our children—where we're going to be. You know, uprooting and looking at a transition from being that working person you've been for the last forty or fifty years and now having a different phase of it.

"I'm looking at that, and my wife and I have talked about having a plant nursery. We want to look at some places where there's a different quality of life, as we go into that next phase. I'm sure my mind will be preoccupied with looking into the future and making certain that the legacy that she and I have developed as parents is safeguarded and protected and passed on to our next generation."

Asked if that means relocation, Martin says, "Most definitely; a relocation or a partial relocation. People have summer homes and winter homes. The Northeast can be a bit treacherous during the wintertime, and we're getting to an age where it's not fun to be under house arrest for six months during the winter. We want to enjoy a twelve-month, outdoor, active life."

I'd read where Martin had traveled through all fifty states, an amazing achievement. Naturally, I wondered if any one of them held an irresistible allure that would place it above the others as his No. 1 dream place. "They all have their unique character," he says. "They all have their own personality. I mean that, literally. But California, to me, has the most diversity as a state. It has mountain ranges, it has deserts, oceanfront, a national forest, and redwood trees. I mean, it just reeks with diversity. Although I grew up there, it's a state I have a great affinity for."

The fraternity of people who have walked the country is a small one, to be sure, and you know right off that you're in the company of some pretty heavy hitters—people like Lewis and Clark, not to mention hundreds of Old West settlers, many of whom in all likelihood "hoofed" it. It hit me that Martin one day might enjoy sitting down and sharing mutual grand experiences with fellow cross-country walking contemporaries Peter Jenkins, the author of *A Walk Across America* in the 1970s, and former Tennessee Governor Lamar Alexander, now a U.S. Senator, who in 1978 walked across the state wearing a red-and-black plaid shirt to connect with the citizenry—a thousand-mile trek.

"Yeah, that's one of the things that my mind has wandered towards," says Martin. "Having those individuals with like interests and like accomplishments to sit down and share those experiences and extract the similarities as well as the differences from that experience. That, to me, places you in elite company. It also broadens your experience to say, 'Yeah, it was the right thing that we experienced, it was the right feeling.' It validates what you've done, so absolutely."

Chapter Three

TALES FROM THE ROAD

As Lee Reeves mentioned, a million stories arise from such a venture, encompassing all categories. From funny to fearsome, bad weather to the patently weird, heartwarming human interest to obstacles overcome—a little bit of everything can and will happen on a trip of this magnitude. Reeves recalls what he still views as the Journey's most bizarre incident, an almost surreal instance that occurred early on, in Maryland right before the team arrived at the 40 Bridge.

"A guy passes us on the side of the road, and he's in a tuxedo," Reeves begins. "He and his assistant passed us as we were going down this hill. They honk the horn and give a friendly wave like everybody else. They do a U-ee, come back, and pull us over. They explain who they are and ask if there is anything they can do—I don't know if they made a donation or not. The guy says, 'If you don't mind, I'd like to do this trick for you.' So he does a card trick right there on the side of the highway. Here we are on a four-lane, and a magician on the side of the road, in his tux, in full regalia, is doing magic tricks for us!"

And then there was the little lady in Virginia, whom Reeves nicknamed after a popular TV show from the mid-1980s, who sailed beyond the point of casual interest in following the Journey team. "Her name was Sylvia," he says. "I call her the 'A-Team,' because she'd pull up in this van, like the old *A-Team* van—you know how the doors would open and they'd rush out of the car? The first time I met her, there were these state troopers that had pulled us over who knew we were in the area. They were asking where George was and wanted to take a picture.

"All of a sudden, this van pulls up, slams on the brakes, the door slides open, and this little old lady runs out and goes, 'There you are!' I'm thinking she's talking to the police—we're in the middle of Virginia. No, she's talking to George Diaz, our EMT! She had met him the day before, and now she goes up and hugs him and says, 'Where's George?' meaning Big George. Every day she'd track us on the computer. She brought bottles of water, introduced her grandkids, her kids—three generations of them—every day for about two weeks when we were in that area."

While fresh stories percolate all the time on the trip, other aspects were carved long ago in stone from familiar association. One such vital element on the trek is Dianne Martin's vigilant monitoring of her husband's well-being, including diet, a topic she's had a bit of experience with.

"I've been doing that for thirty years," says Dianne, a pretty and intelligent woman, of the time spent watching Martin's diet. "Last night he had steak. Every now and then he has to eat like that, but that's very heavy for him. For dinner, usually it's chicken, fish, salads, vegetables. For breakfast he'll have cold cereal and some fruit. Then for lunch he'll have a light sandwich or a salad."

Martin will change clothes for health and comfort during the course of a day, too. "He gets soaking wet; he sweats a lot," she says. "When you're out there and it's cold and you're sweating, you really get cold and stiff. So he'll take a couple of changes [of clothing] with him and change in the car." Dianne referred back to our lunchtime conversation at the motel in Cookeville, when we were waiting for Martin to come down from his room. "Now, since he came in and took a hot shower, he'll feel a lot better," Dianne says. "He'll probably get another twelve or fifteen miles in today."

The early bird's got nothing on Martin, who rises each morning at 5:30 and takes a hot shower to loosen up. "That gets him in the frame of mind to walk," says Dianne. The SUV departs the motel at 6 a.m. to drive to their destination, and they start walking as soon as it gets light. "He has always been a morning man," adds Dianne, who references her husband's earlier training days at Bear Mountain State Park as solid preparation for where he is on the Journey today. "It had the mountains," she says of the park, "which was nice. It kind of prepared him for those inclines here. That was a heck of a workout. He thought, *This is really preparing me well.* But you know, when you're walking it every single day, trying to get in fifteen, twenty, thirty miles, you can't really prepare for that."

To the point where the team is now, in Cookeville, Tennessee, Martin was averaging twenty-two miles per day. "Which isn't bad," Dianne says.

Getting to the Journey

It's a long way from Giants Stadium in the Meadowlands to the cracked shoulder of a secondary highway in central Tennessee. Literally *and* figuratively. For Martin, this improbable trek wasn't in the remote realm of consideration while growing up in Greenville, South Carolina, where his dad sharecropped a twenty-five-acre plot of land. When he was seven, the family headed west, a transcontinental relocation to Fairfield, California, where Martin starred in sports at Armijo High School (1967-71), just east of Napa. He served as student body president, a leadership position that would help prepare him to represent every player in the NFL some years later. It was also at Armijo where he met the future Mrs. George Martin.

"Yep, we were high school sweethearts," acknowledges Martin fondly. "I played high school football and basketball and tennis." The latter may come as a shock to viewers accustomed to seeing the huge numerals seventy-five on a New York Giants uniform. "That's why she and I have a love of tennis to this day."

After graduation, the Martins headed for the University of Oregon, where George majored in art education and played basketball and football. During his junior year in Eugene, the two were married. "Those were real formative years together for Dianne and me," he says.

It was also at Oregon where Martin met a man destined to be a legend and with whom he would have an uncommon connection more than thirty years later. Martin held a high regard for fellow Duck athlete Steve Prefontaine, the celebrated distance runner whose life and distinguished career on the track came quickly to a halt with his untimely death in a car crash at age twenty-four. The world-class runner's days in Eugene overlapped Martin's stay there for a few years, with his death occurring during Martin's senior year. Quoted on those days in a 2007 article by the *New York Times'* Dave Anderson, Martin said:

"When I was at Oregon, I always admired Steve Prefontaine. You'd see him running everywhere all over the campus, not just in track meets. It was as if Steve had a personal affair with nature. I won't be running, but when I'm walking across the country, I'll be thinking of him."

The shared bond with nature and the outdoors was another thread connecting the two Oregon athletes. Throughout the cross-country walk, Martin has professed his good fortune at being able to combine the two greatest passions in his life: a love of nature/outdoor activity and giving back to the community. The fact that he's getting to do both on this quest is an undeniable bonus.

"Lee will sometimes bring me back to reality," Martin says. "He'll say, 'I can see in your eyes that you are enjoying this beyond compare.' I say it takes me back to my childhood, it takes me back to a time of innocence, a time of just wonderment. I said in the *New York Post* article [November 18, 2007] that every day I wake up, I see a beautiful sunrise, I see a magnificent sunset, and that's God's gift to us. It's never been a rerun. Even though we see it every day, it's something different each time, it's something unique, and I count that as a blessing. I really do."

Truly, it's difficult to imagine how anyone could embark on a journey of this nature and not come away changed. "Oh my goodness," Martin says, still counting those blessings. "And that's one of the things that I hoped for and had wished for, and it's coming true. Every day it comes true."

Though his collegiate career with the Ducks produced no particular notoriety on the field, Giants scouts were well aware of Martin's superior physical assets and upside. His work was still cut out for him after draft day, when New York selected him with its eleventh-round pick, but the Giants were right in their initial assessment: Martin was a keeper, in fact the *only* keeper from the Giants draft class of 1975. No other player selected by New York that year played more than three years with the Giants.

Back when Martin joined the team, New York was pathetic, having logged just two winning seasons in the twelve years separating Martin's rookie campaign in 1975 from the last of the great Giants teams of the late 1950s and early '60s—the 1963 NFL Championship Game finalists. But it would be another seven seasons after Martin's arrival in New York before the Giants posted the first winning season of Martin's fourteen-year stay in the Big Apple, and it wasn't until his tenth season (and second under head coach Bill Parcells) that New York's fortunes finally began to take a turn for the better.

Though he stayed to play for two more years, he in essence capped his career with the 39–20 Super Bowl XXI victory over

Denver in 1986, in which he downed Broncos quarterback John Elway for a crucial safety in the second period. At the time, the Giants were down 10–7. The two-point score reenergized the New Yorkers, who then went on a 30–10 scoring run to win going away.

"The year that we won the Super Bowl we played the Denver Broncos in the regular season," Martin, then a Giants tri-captain, recalls. "I had intercepted a pass and ran it back seventy-eight yards for a touchdown, if you can believe that. It's documented, so it really did happen."

The play, a one-handed grab and runback of an Elway pass, was later called by coach Parcells the "greatest football play I've ever seen." Martin paused his reply but not his pace for a moment, inhaling a huge lungful of late-November country air. "My dad happened to be at that Denver game. You talk about being fortuitous, he witnessed that. And I kept that game ball, and it was a great honor to present it to him. That was one of the highlights, and then also later that year, we actually won the Super Bowl. And there again, John Elway played a big role in that, because I tackled him in the end zone for a safety. The only safety of my career, and it happened in the Super Bowl—and my dad was there once again. Those are two very special highlights in my career on the field."

Prior to that, Martin had distinguished himself by ringing up an inordinate number of touchdowns for a defensive end. Six to be exact, an NFL career record for defensive linemen (since broken by Miami Dolphins defensive end Jason Taylor). Martin actually recorded a total of seven touchdowns in his career, including a scoring reception when he lined up as a tight end in a 1980 game.

In addition to his solid on-field presence, Martin, along with teammate Harry Carson, was a locker room leader, a voice of strength and resolve who commanded the respect of his peers. Parcells again exalted him, once calling Martin "a pillar of locker-room leadership."

It is suggested that the former Giants defensive stalwart must be in far greater shape today from his Forrest Gumping it across

America than when he was sweating it out under Parcells's rigorous two-a-days back in summer camp.

"I'm not sure; that might be questionable," Martin considers. "Bill Parcells was pretty demanding during two-a-days, but this has been no less demanding. And I think, myself and Lee, that we've been kind of amazed at the terrain that we've encountered, and we seem to have conquered it with relative ease so far, and I'm pleased." The recollection and comparison trigger a last thought on the subject from Martin: "I don't know, though," he says smiling, "back then, Bill Parcells said I played five years *beyond* my prime."

For A Journey for 9/11 to get off the ground, it was essential that Martin get a leave of absence from his job as vice president of sports marketing for AXA Equitable. Good things happened right off the bat. Company officials Andrew McMahon and Nick Lane not only granted Martin's request but extended it, with pay. As mentioned earlier, Martin knew Lee Reeves from their days with MONY before the financial giant was purchased by AXA, a Paris-based company that also had purchased Equitable when that company was in financial trouble, becoming AXA Equitable.

"He and I go back," Reeves says. "Me, twenty-five years, and I think him, twenty years with MONY. Again, they're AXA now. He refers to them as AXA, but his whole twenty-five years was not with them."

Next a slew of sponsors were solicited, coming on board to help underwrite the Journey's considerable expenses, and a Web site—www.ajourneyfor911.info—was established to begin the huge job of informing the public of the venture and of setting up an online means for people to track Martin's progress across the country as well as make donations. In addition, General Electric donated the previously mentioned RV.

Reeves had his own obstacle course to negotiate before joining the Journey team. He was at a crossroads in his career when Martin first talked to him about the cross-country walk. Unsure whether he wished to continue in the financial world, Reeves went to an AXA Equitable senior vice president, who gave him an exit package that allowed him to leave.

"If it wasn't for that," admits Reeves, "I couldn't do this."

What he did do was create his own company. "I started a technology firm several months ago, and we handle all of the technology for A Journey for 9/11," Reeves says. He charges Martin about a third of what normally would be charged for a project of this size and nature. "Plus, I'm out here 100 percent of my time, dedicated to doing this," he says, "so I can't do other business right now." The adventurous prospect initially caused Reeves to dip into his investments and liquidate some of his holdings. "That's how much this meant to me," he says. When Martin asked if Reeves would join the Journey team, Reeves told him yes.

"And when he talked to me about using my firm to handle the technology, they didn't have any money," says Reeves. "There was no money coming in, but I said, 'I'll do it. I have four employees who will work on this.' Jennifer [Skor] is one of the employees, who was working full time, no pay. I told George, 'When you can afford to pay me, pay me.' But for right now, I'm financing it out of investments. When I told Jennifer that I was going to have her work on this project, she said, 'Okay, cut my salary in half.' And when she gets her first check, she's going to donate that back to Journey. Her husband works for GE [a sponsor of A Journey for 9/11], and GE is going to match that donation. But as of right now, Jennifer has not received one penny. But again, this is a testament to George's passion and leadership and belief in this program. One day, when they can afford to pay me, they'll pay me, and things will be great, but I'm not worried about that."

It is suggested that Reeves and his associates' actions are noble under the circumstances. "The nobility is on his [Martin's] part," Reeves quickly interjects, "because I would have never thought to do anything like this."

That's not to say that the massive endeavor has been a walk in the park for Reeves. "Let me tell you, the biggest inconvenience for me is my fiancée and I: We worked together, we took lunches together, we took breaks together. I mean, we were never separated by more than a day since we've been together, and that's years. For us to be away from each other for this long a period of time is the *only* sacrifice I'm making." Reeves's fiancée, Flor DeJesus, works in New York City, but the pair have a home. "I had just bought a home that I fell in love with," he says of the house purchased in August 2006, "so that's a tough part, too, being away from there."

Safety first

To begin the rigorous ordeal of training, Martin began walking from his home in Ringwood, New Jersey, to Bear Mountain State Park in New York thirteen miles away, then pacing off another dozen miles inside the park. Dianne usually picked him up at that point for the ride back home. But physical training for the Journey was only one part of the overall preparation. Scads of details and logistical elements had to be addressed, for this would *not* be a walk across America via its interstate highway system. The complexities of gaining access to the superhighway infrastructure were myriad, and the lack of safety was a whole other matter. The mere thought of attempting to cross the country on interstates drew shivers from Reeves.

"There would be no way you could guarantee your safety," he said unhesitatingly. "Those eighteen-wheelers flying by at eighty within a yard or two of you? No way."

So, the troupe takes to the secondary roads, the old two- and four-lane blacktops that wind through the country like a serpentine Yellow Brick Road. They were going to experience the majesty of making their way cross-country like travelers of earlier generations, who followed such hallowed paths as old Route 66 to their ultimate destinations.

Yet, danger is no stranger to the federal and state highway grids either. From the outset, "safety first" has been the rule and rallying cry of the Journey for 9/11 team. The reason is simple: whether on an interstate highway or a backcountry lane, something awfully wrong can happen awfully fast.

"Let me tell you. We were in Virginia, walking down a high-way—there's no shoulder. What you see here would be gracious," Reeves says, pointing to the uneven edge of U.S. 70 on which we were walking. "It was a four-lane highway, two on each side, and a lady stopped to give a donation. George said to me, 'Go over and talk to her,' so I walk across a huge median, down a ditch-like ravine, and across two more lanes of traffic to talk to this lady. Then I see George coming behind me. I'm like, 'George, just keep walk-ing, I got this.' But he insisted on coming over. All of the sudden, you hear screeching brakes. An eighteen-wheeler runs off the road, right where we were walking!"

I mention that it sounds like some fantastical video game, a scene of potentially deadly disaster miraculously averted.

"This lady that I saw as an inconvenience—me having to go over and talk to her—probably prevented us from being in the path of an eighteen-wheeler," Reeves remarks, still incredulous at the good fortune that came their way. "Talk about a video game! Then, I don't know what happened."

After the interaction with the woman, Martin told his EMT George Diaz to get out of the car and walk with him. "Now I'm out of the car, and we go maybe fifty or a hundred feet, and again, you hear these screeching tires, and then you hear *BAM!*" recalls Reeves. "We had no idea what it was. So we walked a little further. Not much longer we wrapped it up for the day, got in the car, did a U-ee coming back home, and found out that the second incident was yet another eighteen-wheeler hitting a dump truck. You just had a wall of dirt after that. So, had they been out walking on that side, they would have just gotten flattened. There was nowhere to go."

Out of such frightening incidents strategic plans are born. "We always look for our exit strategy," confirms Reeves. "We'll say, 'You're going to jump over that guardrail,' or 'You're going to do this,' or 'You're going to do that.' Sometimes, there's just no place to go. So when you talk about it being like a video game, you don't know how close to home you're hitting."

Dianne Martin, though her role as A Journey for 9/11's media coordinator mostly places her back at the motel during the daytime hours, remembers one accident that resulted from people just not using their heads. "The team was walking along the road," she says, "when this lady pulls up and stops right in the lane. She says, 'Are you guys those ones that I saw—' and she was going to say 'on TV' when somebody rear-ended her. She had a baby in the back seat and she got hysterical. George or Lee didn't even have time to say 'Pull up.'

"People do that all the time; they're not even thinking; they just see the team, and they're 'Oh, that's those guys,' and then they'll stop right in the middle of the road. The team will say 'Pull over and we'll talk to you,' or 'Come to the next intersection, and we'll talk to you and take pictures.' But before they could even say anything, she was rear-ended. She was okay and the baby was okay. Just one instance of not thinking."

Congested traffic and impatient drivers bunching up behind Martin always pose a serious safety threat, and at those times extra vigilance is mandatory. "The worst is when you have cars trying to get around us," notes Reeves. "We will try and stop the cars, because they're on an incline or on a curve, and we can see that there are other cars coming. George will put his hands out, flagging them to stop, and they'll go right around. I can't tell you how many close calls we've had like that. The cars take one of two options: They either hit the oncoming traffic head-on, or they swerve back over into the lane where the walkers are. So it's not just about the walk. You look at the walk and the physicality of that, and you think, 'Man, that's commitment.' But you've got to realize, George has got his life in his hands every day."

I mention to Lee that previously I had been under the misapprehension that the Journey for 9/11 team's route for traversing the nation was the major east-west conveyor known as I-40. When you hear scary tales from the road, such as those being rendered by Reeves, you begin to ponder what a crossing like that would really be like, and there is only one inescapable conclusion to come to: It would be harrowing.

"You've seen cars drive forty or fifty miles an hour going through here," says Reeves. "Now, imagine eighteen-wheelers passing you at seventy-five or eighty-five miles an hour, roaring by within probably ten feet of you. All you'd need is a blowout and the entire team is toast, or to have someone hit this flank car from behind and knock the flank car into you. The irony is that—and I don't know if this is good luck or bad luck—generally the individuals, the citizens, the residents, are stopping us on a regular basis, like the father-and-son combination you saw back there a while ago on their bikes. They're stopping *all* day. It's 'Who are you? What are you about?' That's the reason George put together this kit." Reeves shows a small brochure that includes a donation card. "We can hand this to them," he says. "It explains it, rather than us having to stand there for fifteen to twenty minutes and explain the whole purpose of the Journey to them."

Reeves pauses a moment, reflecting on the current stage. "But this is the least activity I think I've seen since we've been in the state of Tennessee." It will be nothing, I tell him, compared to the vast, barren stretches of the Texas Panhandle, or beyond, in New Mexico and Arizona.

Chapter Four

RAISING THE JOURNEY FOR 9/11

D onations, lying at the heart of the trip, certainly occupy a high spot on the ladder of priorities for the Journey for 9/11 team. The goal initially was to raise ten million dollars, but that later was scaled back to "several million dollars," and Martin stresses that every dollar helps. As of press time for this book (June 2008), the team had generated $2,002,031. One thing about the money being raised on this mission for the first responders is that any level of donation is prized and revered. While walking at one point with George and Lee, both took turns telling tell me a story about picking up change.

"He has a jar that he's keeping it in," says Lee. "There's a story behind it. We have a motto about passing up change."

"We both come from a similar background," says Martin about Reeves and himself. "We don't pass up money. We're not so proud that we wouldn't bend to pick up a penny. A penny is a penny. It really is. That's my philosophy. A penny here, a penny there—pretty soon you're talking about real money." Martin then gets to the heart of it. "It's hard for us to ask for money if you pass up change lying on the ground. That would be a contradiction of why we're out here and what we're about. People say, 'Well that's not a lot of money,' but to me that penny is representative of something larger. It really is."

So many of the values inherent in other eras of innocence seem lost today. You used to put a quarter under a kid's pillow for a tooth. Now they want five bucks.

George laughs. "Yeah, something that folds. They're not ashamed to tell you, too."

Lee notes that Dianne is the keeper of the change jar. "What's the record, George, eighty-nine cents in a day?"

"Nine dollars in a day."

I'm shocked. "*Yeah*," Lee says. "We thought we were going to have a shutout yesterday. I found a penny earlier in the day. I think he found, what, eleven cents maybe? How much, George?"

"Two cents."

"Yeah 'cause the other one was not a dime after all. We ended up with three pennies yesterday," sums up Reeves. "But it goes in the jar, and then at the end of the Journey, it will go *into* the Journey."

"When you reach the Golden Gate Bridge, George," I say, "I hope you find a big ol' hundred-dollar bill right there on the ground."

Martin laughs. "You can always go ahead of us and plant it. What did Benjamin Franklin say? 'A penny saved . . .'"

". . . 'Is a penny earned.'"

"Yep. And if I'm going to go out and ask for contributions and make requests, you know what? I can't be so proud as to not be able to pick up a penny," says Martin. "That could make a difference in somebody's life!"

Reeves then produces a magnificent instance of multiple coins in action. "The kids from one of the Charter Schools gave us 911 gold coins," Lee says. It is a tale that Reeves and Dianne Martin both vote as the best story thus far on their travels.

"That's the one I'll remember the most," say Reeves, of the Journey team's experience at Friendship Public Charter School in Washington, D.C. "We were pulling up, and George happened to be driving the Journey bus. This big bus pulls up and the kids see it and start screaming, 'There he is! There he is!' You open the door for George to step out, and a marching band greets us! Young inner-city children were there, the band plays, and the dance group comes out and performs 'Ease On Down the Road.' They presented him with 911 Susan B. Anthony dollar coins. Of all the things—we were on Capitol Hill, there were so many things—but that one, that one I'll never forget."

Donations vary wildly in scope, from a penny all the way up to a check for $911,000. It is a humbling thing, and Reeves, in observing the always grateful appreciation expressed by Martin at those times, comes away with more head-shaking admiration for his friend.

"You talk about somebody's personality and character," says Reeves, "We had one lady who gave a dollar. She felt so bad, because all she had in her pocket was a dollar. George took as much time with that lady that gave a dollar as he did with a lady that gave $400. That to me speaks to his character."

Martin feels their brochure has been an invaluable aid in helping raise money. "I think you've seen evidence of it, the gentlemen we just met," says Martin, referring to the father-son cyclists we had encountered early in the afternoon. "We give them a pamphlet, and the pamphlet tells in detail what A Journey for 9/11 really is. But inclusive in that is also a contribution sheet, a donation sheet, and they can elect to donate in a number of ways: They can zip it right into the bank, or they can go online and pay, or there's a toll-free number they can call to make a contribution.

"We do rely heavily upon our sponsors; they come through in grand fashion. We're very pleased with the people we've aligned ourselves with, and inclusive in that obviously is the NFL, who committed $50,000 to A Journey for 9/11 and another $5,000 in maximum funds, so we're very pleased with who's represented in this journey."

Beginning a slight incline heading west along Highway 70/96, the old Nashville Highway, the Journey crew passes through an area where Bug Hunt and the two Edwards boys once held up the Cookeville-Nashville stagecoach at midnight on an October night in 1882. Hunt later was captured and jailed. A Tennessee Historical Commission marker bills the event as the *last* stagecoach holdup. George and I had been talking about the effects of gratitude and how it is now being connected to better health. Recent study findings indicate that when we show appreciation, good things happen to our bodies.

"I'll give you an example, if you don't mind," George says. "The guys always precede me when we go into a restaurant or to the hotel, and I kind of keep a low profile. I'll stay in the car at such times, so as not to create a stir. The other day they came back and said, 'George, this gentleman gave us five bucks at the hotel.' The man thought that Lee was me. He said, 'I been waiting to meet you, it's a real pleasure, an honor,' and Lee says, 'No, wait till you meet the big guy, you can't miss him,' and the man says, 'Here's a contribution to the Journey, here's five bucks,' which he'd gotten from his girlfriend.

"Well, when we came in later that day, the guys introduced me to him. Lee says, 'See the difference between him and me? This is George Martin.' And I said, 'I heard you made a contribution to our cause. We really appreciate it. It's something that gets us motivated.' We made a big deal of it, not because we thought it was something he would like; we did it because he was being genuine. The next day I came downstairs and walked past the front desk. The young lady there says, 'Mr. Martin, there's an envelope here for you.' I said, "Okay thanks,' and put it in my jacket pocket. I didn't think anything about it.

"Later, my wife says, 'You know, there's money in that envelope.' I said, 'How do you know?' She says, 'Listen, I've been married to you for thirty-five years, I know the look of that.' I open it up. And there's $400 in it—four one-hundred-dollar bills! It was from the man's girlfriend, who had seen how we responded to the five-dollar contribution. She had a wonderful note on the envelope. It said: 'This is just for making us feel like special people.' You can't say anything after that. She didn't leave an address; she didn't want to be recognized. It was almost like an anonymous donation."

It's funny how, when people are truly giving, they tend to give in such a way that it can't be repaid.

"Exactly," says George. "And that's exactly what she did."

Bountiful blessings include a check for $911,000 from Carol and Joseph Reich. When the couple learned of Martin's plans, they were quick to respond financially. "My wife and I supported the 9/11 Foundation when it started," Reich has said. "We were both upset at the way the federal and local government failed to treat real American heroes. When we saw what George was doing, we called him and told him that what he was doing was extraordinary."

And then there is the heartwarming story of the Beets family. If you were to take a microcosm of American life, of the way we all would like to be treated and welcomed by strangers, you'd have to go a long way to find a better example than what happened in tiny Rogersville, Tennessee, on October 26, 2007.

It was toward the end of the day as the troupe passed through the little hamlet that lies roughly thirty miles west of Kingsport, one of the Tri Cities hubs. George, bone-weary tired, had asked Dianne if she'd mind ordering dinner for them all.

"We come across this big sign that says, 'Pig and Chick.' That tells you: pork," says Reeves, again alluding to the omnipresence of that delightful Southern staple to which they had all been overwhelmingly exposed on the course of their walk. "I look at George and he looks at me and we both say, 'No.' Coincidentally, it was there that we elected to call it a day. It was a great landmark, 'Pig and Chick,' so we'll start the next day there. Suddenly, this woman comes running out the door and says, 'Come in! Come in!' So we're wondering, *Okay, what is this about?* The woman says, 'I want to buy you dinner.' Again, George can't say no. He was tired, it was the end of the day, he wanted to go home, he'd asked Dianne to order dinner . . . and now this woman invites us in. He couldn't say no. He calls Dianne and tells her to cancel. We go in to eat, and the woman refuses to allow us to pay."

George and Lee have this thing they do, always trying to one-up the other for the check. Now George looks at his friend, with the thought of turning the tables on their gracious host, and says, "Lee, you know that game we play all the time? Let's play it now."

At that, Reeves heads for the register, while their table mate and newfound friend is still breaking bread.

"I say to the young lady at the desk, 'I need to take care of the check from the table,'" says Reeves. "The lady says, 'I can't take your money. The owners are on their way. They know you're here and they want to treat you to the meal.'"

Two sets of folks now trying to pick up their tab. Reeves goes back to the table and tells the woman, whose name is Belinda, "We were going to one-up you and pay for the meal, but the owners are on their way and they want to treat us." Soon after, the owners came in.

"It was a blast," recalls Reeves. "The young lady who had invited us in? Her mom showed up. They had scheduled dinner together that night there at the place. The owners, Richard and Marti Beets, both came in and they treated us. The city judge was there that night, too. He came over, and all of a sudden out of that came the keys to the city of Rogersville, because Marti Beets had introduced us to the local politicians and the chief of police!"

I mention that it seemed like the folks in Rogersville got it all together in a hurry. "It was like that," Lee says emphatically, snapping his fingers. "Overnight! So they ended up sure enough treating us to dinner that night. They had a ceremony the next day, where they presented us with the keys to the city, and George went by one of the schools. Wouldn't you know, little George, the EMT, has a dental problem. Dianne had made elaborate plans to get him to a dental office but had canceled those plans. I was saying to the Beets, 'You know, George Diaz, has got a dental problem. Do you have a dentist you can recommend us to?'

"Not only did Marti Beets know a dentist," he marvels, "she called him immediately. The dentist prescribed some medication for George, and she went and picked it up. She also paid for the medication and brought the medication back, absolutely *refusing* to take any money. She then called ahead to Knoxville and scheduled surgery, in case an extraction was needed, and would not take a penny. Would not take a penny!"

"The next day, when we were on our way out of town, that's when I met them," says Dianne of her first meeting with the Beetses, "because I had not been on the road the night before. George said, 'We're going by this place for lunch, because they said we'd have to pass right by them and to come in for lunch.' Well, they don't normally open early, but we got there like at ten in the morning. They opened for us. They had their *whole menu* ready for whatever we wanted to eat that day. We had lunch with them and talked a little bit more, and then they sent us on our way."

Fighting misconceptions

If exceptional hospitality is indeed the hallmark of a proud South, then the Beets family carried it to the next level with their unsolicited and warm show of generosity and loving kindness to the Journey for 9/11 team. The fact that it happened in the South is even better. It may well be the year 2008, but that doesn't mean that African Americans from the South still wouldn't be a bit apprehensive about taking a stroll through their homeland. Dianne, Lee,

and George know full well the region's history of racial tension, dis-
sension, and violence, especially native sons of the South George, a
South Carolinian, and Lee, who was born in Jackson, Tennessee.

"When we were first starting out, us being African-American
people, we thought, *Going through the South . . . all these black people
walking on the side of the road . . . how safe is that going to be?*"
remembers Dianne. "But it has been the total opposite. People have
been just so nice. They stop and offer drinks, you know, 'Do you
need bottles of water?' They give one or two dollars, and in this area
that's a lot of money. You realize this is a very depressed area, and
people don't have that much for them to give one or two dollars.
And they all apologize, because they can't give any more. It's very
heartwarming."

George echoed his wife's sentiments, saying he'd experienced the
same anxiety that Dianne and Lee had as the team drew nearer to the
South. But afterward, Martin would log it as one of the new percep-
tions gained from his experience of walking across the country.

"I've got to be honest and say, having been born here and
growing up in the segregated South during the nineteen fifties
and sixties, I didn't think I would be met with open arms in the
deep heart of the South," Martin says candidly. "It was a staggering surprise, an absolute staggering surprise of epic propor-
tion, to see how these people have, from every walk of life,
embraced us. I had one guy, a big ol' jolly-looking fella, come
over, and he said, 'Come on into my store, I'm going to feed
you. I'm going to set you some food out!' I thanked the man
very much and extended my hand to shake his hand, but he says,
'Oh, no,' and gave me this big bear hug, like we were long-lost
brothers. I was floored.

"Remember when the guy on the bicycle talked about the difference between the big communities and the smaller communities?
I found that to be true. The people with the very least to give have
given the most proportionally. And they do it with such passion,

they do it with such *love*, they just make you feel like a million bucks. And then they apologize because they don't have more to give! That, to me, is phenomenal."

Lee Reeves relates a relevant tale of potential scariness that had recently occurred near the Virginia-Tennessee border. "There was one story," he begins. "We were on the highway in Virginia, when some officers warned us about certain areas, saying when we got into this area, we really needed to be cognizant, to be aware, meaning we were two black men traveling in this rural area where there's known to be problems. We get up there and encounter some of these people they had been talking about, and of course, they couldn't have been friendlier. I even have photos of George with some of the very people they were warning us about.

"Then we get into Tennessee, and we have a similar kind of experience, where they were telling us the names of the cities. I don't want to repeat them, but they gave us three cities, and they said, 'When you get into this area, this area, and *this* area—we don't care what your experiences were in Virginia—when you get into these places, you need to be aware of good ol' *yay-hoos* down there. They're not used to seeing you out there.'

"So sure enough, we're walking through the area, and I think it was a county sheriff, maybe, pulled us over and wanted to take a picture with George. So I took a shot, and George and I walked on down the road and left George Diaz behind in the SUV. Once we left, the police officer said, 'You know, I'm amazed we haven't gotten any calls from the local residents, 'cause we don't get colored people down here.' But everywhere we've gone and every place they've warned us about—knock on wood—we've had great experiences. It's such a great story. It's an American story. It's not a black story. It's not a white story. It's an American story."

As a Tennessee resident, I tell them, it's good to hear such things. No one wants to find out that the citizenry of one's own state would mistreat beautiful people on such a noble mission.

"As a native Tennessean, I sure didn't want to hear that," Reeves adds. "I mean, I know pockets like that exist, but they exist in New York, they exist all over the country. To hear them say be careful in those areas didn't surprise me. What I didn't want to do was add any negative experiences, because I've been bragging to George since we got here about how people have been so receptive to us, and I just didn't want to see anything like that come up. And, fortunately, it has not. Hopefully, we'll continue to tread throughout the state and throughout the country and continue to see what we've seen so far."

Interestingly, later, Martin, when talking about football, used an analogy citing the Journey team's initial misapprehension about walking through the rural South due to the contemptible actions of a small segment of Southerners in the past. In much the same manner, many people today observing the NFL from the outside misperceive its character, primarily seeing it through the negative attention-getting antics of a few.

"I think some young athletes today are under the gross misconception that what they are as professional athletes is who they are," says Martin of the league's bad apples. "Nothing could be further from the truth, and the reality is, as soon as they take that uniform from you, you'll find out what your true makeup is. It's unfortunate they have to find out the hard way."

Chapter Five

ANTI-TERRORISM
IN THE
TENNESSEE HILLS

The walkie-talkie beeps. "That's a warning that a car's coming," Lee explains. "Rather than just flank us in the car, George and Daren are actually ahead, watching traffic. They call on the radio every time a vehicle comes by, especially a wide load." Seconds later, the unit beeps again. "Disregard" crackles a voice over the radio.

About a hundred yards head, Martin suddenly stops. Reeves smiles; he knows what's coming.

"He's a country boy," Reeves says of his friend with affection. "He's seen something up there that he loves." Martin signals for them to bring the camera. "He loves barns," says Reeves, "but only the ones that are falling down." The camera has decided to hide among the jackets, provisions, and other loose flotsam within the flank vehicle. "Is it back here?" A door beeps, left ajar, as the car's occupants file out to meet with Martin. "I have no idea where it is," says Reeves, still unflappable. Finally locating the camera, he grabs it and vacates the car now parked along the roadside.

It is a photo op. Martin has spied a jaw-dropping vista, and everyone convenes for a group shot in front of the scenic backdrop. "You can't tell me you don't stop to smell the roses, George," I say to Martin, as we wait for George Diaz to shoot the picture. Lee laughs, "He *always* finds time."

The driver of a car heading in the opposite direction eyes the team, then pulls to a quick stop just past the group gathered alongside the eastbound guardrail. A woman in her late thirties or early forties rushes from the vehicle, a wad of papers clutched wildly in one hand, and breathlessly heads toward the Journey team.

The woman introduces herself as Patra Minocha. Working out of Cookeville, Tennessee, she was traveling her normal route to and from work, when she spotted the Journey team. "I'm into fighting terrorism big time," she announces to Reeves, who is the first to intercept her. "I've got all kinds of anti-terrorist poster ideas. I have not done the artwork for these, but this is an eighteen-by-twenty-four-inch sign . . . ," the woman says, diving into her pitch, clearly oblivious that her new audience might have its own agenda. Reeves handles the situation with patience and professionalism, introducing the immediate cast around him.

"This is wonderful! How long have you been walking?" Minocha inquires.

"September sixteenth. We left the George Washington Bridge in New York City," recounts Reeves. "We're trying to take care of the first responders." He points up the road. That's George Martin from the New York Giants.

"Oh, wow, I've got to show him something," the woman says, the wheels already churning in her head. "Is that football or basketball?"

"Football," answers Reeves. "Yes."

"Look at what I'm doing now," says Minocha, rummaging hastily through her horde of papers. "Look, look, I'm trying to get the Super Bowl of Blessings going. I've been in Pepsi Cola's North

America office, I've got one more image to be made." She points to a page among her clutch, rotating it right-side-up for Reeves to see. "This is taken from an NFL Experience book, I'm going to have to get their names off of here for legal reasons, but [the artist] put seven Pepsis in their hands. It's supposed to be the Super Bowl of Blessings."

With lightning speed, Minocha changes direction. "I broke my hip several months ago. I have a rod in here, so I feel like I can do anything now, overcoming that," she points out, as she feverishly rifles through a quagmire of posters and pages of cause-related materials, her cache looking like a spread-out fan that at any moment could be swept from her grasp by the wind and lofted into the hills like so many pieces of paper hail. Relentlessly, the woman surges on.

"Here it is, the Super—I'd love to hear what you are doing—Super Bowl of Blessings: Scoring touchdowns, tackle drugs . . . ," Minocha reads on. It is a delicate situation for the 9/11 team. With perhaps only another hour of sunlight remaining, Martin obviously wants to get in some more miles. Balancing that, though, as Reeves pointed out earlier, is an opportunity to "light one candle," to inform one more person about the noble goal of Martin's mission. Their work is cut out for them. It is Minocha doing the informing. Nonstop. "And I want to benefit Teen Challenge and have two hundred Christian-based drug rehab centers in this country and abroad."

"You'd be impressed to know George's role. He was—" Reeves is abruptly cut off by the verbose Minocha.

"Displaced victims of natural disasters, and then there's another one: Teen Challenge is a twelve- to fifteen-month program," she says, before finally turning civil and inquiring about the Journey mission. "I know you're doing great things, but can I do anything advertising-wise to help you?"

Reeves may have felt it was against his better judgment, but nonetheless he calls to Martin, who is resting some distance away, to join the group.

"Let me introduce you to George," Reeves says. "Let me tell you a little bit about his background."

Paying no heed, Minocha bulls ahead: "I've got, like, six different anti-terrorist poster ideas, plus this sign against terrorism . . ."

"We're here to take care of those people who tried to take care of us on 9/11," Reeves begins. "We live in New York." It is a timely instance to hand out the Journey for 9/11 brochure with the donation card. "This is material on who we are and what we're doing; our Web site is here as well. But, let me introduce you to George. George, do you have second? This is George Martin."

The woman looks up and smiles at the former football star. "Nice to meet you, my name is Patra, with Brave Hill Productions. I do public safety campaigns and slogans for billboards—all kinds of stuff. I've got a lot of anti-terrorist ideas. I've got this sign at the Department of Safety and Homeland Security in Nashville right now." She repeats most of what she has just told Reeves and continues to scramble through her jumble of papers. "These are anti-meth things. I've got banners for border patrol. I've got this one; it ties in with what you're doing, too: 'Operation save the nation . . . verifying threats to our homeland and environment.'"

Reeves, beginning to feel the frustration of the one-sided exchange and with an eye on his watch, diplomatically informs the talkative Minocha that Martin and the team need to keep moving on, in hopes of logging more miles before the day ends. The woman is undeterred, spraying the Journey for 9/11 team with her consuming agenda like an Uzi emptying on a crowd of hostile revolutionaries.

"I've been focusing on this for a long time," she incants in Martin's direction. "I'm trying to get the Super Bowl of Blessings going, and I'm going to send this to Pepsi Cola North America, in Purchase, New York, and I'm trying to get them to make bowls—super bowls, that are gigantic bowls, to sell at the Super Bowl game and at Dollar General and Wal-Mart to raise money for Teen

Challenge and for the displaced victims of natural disasters. The Pepsi ad is going to say, 'Players, spectators, and the spectacular taste of Pepsi.'

The clear misuse of the NFL's copyrighted property is a red flag for Martin. "Have you gotten a release from the Miami Dolphins?" he asks, spying the figures of several Miami players in the photo Minocha is displaying.

"I'll get to those things," she says quickly. "It'll be cool. I have to get all of that done. But I've got your information."

Martin turns to renew his walk. "Nice meeting you," he says cordially to the woman.

"God bless you," Minocha replies. "Who are you with again?

"The New York Giants."

"Wow. Is your name in there?" she asks pointing to the Journey brochure. "Where are you going to?"

"We're going to San Francisco," Martin replies. "The Golden Gate Bridge."

"God bless you, God bless your journey."

Reeves also thanks the woman, mentioning that the little caravan has walked almost nine hundred miles now. Minocha begins to rev it up once again. "Can I write my name on something?" She searches for a blank scrap of paper among her disarrayed passel. "I write a lot of stuff that's philanthropic; I've got a lot of stuff that's still dropping. I've got things like this, I've got road signs, I've got anti-drug signs in eleven towns. I've got banners, I've got stuff from here to Montana. I've got these in Montana; I've got stuff in seven states." She produces a pair of illustrations. "This poster is in Montana, and here's an anti-meth poster . . ." Her style is reminiscent of the old barking pitchmen paid to pull people in off the sidewalks, a self-appointed peddler of tonics, elixirs, and jazz.

Admittedly Minocha's energy level and passion for her causes are impressive; she's a veritable whirling dervish, albeit somewhat scattered. "Anti-drug, public safety," she goes on, with rapid-fire precision. "I'm on disability. I was a registered nurse for years, but I've been on disability fifteen or sixteen years. I'm environmentally sensitive, chemically sensitive. God puts these things in your heart. You know, he's doing what you're doing. I'll say this, another slogan I want to get out there is Christian: 'True success is serving the Lord with a compassionate heart, and a courageous soul.'"

"Nicely said," Lee and I both reply.

"I'm just so excited that you're doing this!" Minocha says, in that Ari Gold-like manner that actor Jeremy Piven portrays so well on the hit HBO series *Entourage*. It isn't long before she's changing gears again. "I'd do anything to fight terrorism, anything I can do to help. I'll give, I'll give, I'll give. Did you see the billboard with the eagle on it? Top Flight Financing? That's my slogan; that's my two billboards."

Lee is beeped. Mercifully, he leads us away, but before departing, he turns to the woman, and in his impeccably genial way, says, "Well, as you know, we're here because of terrorism, so those responders are suffering right now, and we're trying to right that wrong."

"We have to bring people to Christ," Minocha responds. "We've got to bring people to God."

"This guy has shared the stage with Billy Graham," Lee says to her, about Martin. "And his religious background, he was very heavily involved with the NFL and Christian leadership."

"It's very bizarre that I come across him when I'm doing something like this, too," she says.

Bizarre. Works for me.

The roadside incident is discussed briefly inside the Trail Blazer. We had just survived a full frontal sales assault from an anti-terrorist. Actually, the experience was a fascinating glimpse into an average day for Lee Reeves, in that sometimes you just don't know from which direction you're going to get hit. The interference that Reeves runs for Martin is inestimable. At the risk of a gratuitous cliché, it's akin to Martin's Super Bowl XXI teammate, fullback

Maurice Carthon, leading the blocking for All-Pro running back Joe Morris back in the day. Reeves is unquestionably committed to his friend's mission, totally giving it his all. Fronting, advancing, teching, coordinating, general managing, and you better believe it, walking. You can tell in any number of responses from him that he is as devoted to this quest as his friend Martin.

"I have to keep him walking at all expense," Reeves says. "He stops, he takes the time. But on a day like today, he's got miles to get behind him. He's really not being rude, but . . . if he met with everyone a half hour, forty-five minutes every time we got stopped, we'd never get to California."

You sense there has to be something very special about a person to make a man talk so protectively about him. The good that runs through someone has to begin somewhere. Martin's interest in helping others, it turns out, took root early, as he watched closely the caring ways of his mother.

COURTESY OF A JOURNEY FOR 9/11

Martin's Journey for 9/11 is a journey of discovery as well, for unusual sights and interesting people abound along the transcontinental route.

The roots of benevolence

"In my teens," Martin begins, "I happened to witness my mom in an act of charity and benevolence. We were poor. I'm telling you, we gave *poor* people a bad name. My mom had fixed this fantastic meal, and I was just so excited—it wasn't a holiday or anything like that. But instead of giving it to us, her five children, she took it across the street to a family that was worse off than we were. The lady she gave it to was brought to tears. I mean, she was speechless. It was a very emotional time, and it galvanized me in that moment. Being a religious person, I believe it is truly better to give than to receive. That was the way I had been all my life."

If you look at the history of George Martin and what he has accomplished off the field, it's easy to pick up the trail of deeds well done. He is a co-founder and executive board member— along with former New York Giants teammates Harry Carson and Ron Johnson—of a not-for-profit organization called Minority Athletes Networking (MAN Etc. Inc.), which is committed to helping inner-city youth. Martin is also an ambassador for the NFL's Youth Football initiative; a board member of the New York Football Giants Alumni, where he helps disenfranchised former team members return to productive roles in society; a former Fairleigh Dickinson University board member; Tomorrows Children's Fund honorary president; and Make-A-Wish Foundation honorary dinner chairman. In addition, Martin was honored with the prestigious Byron "Whizzer" White Humanitarian Award in 1987 and in December 2007 received the Heisman Humanitarian Award, an honor that came with a $25,000 donation to A Journey for 9/11 from the organization that presents the Heisman Trophy to the nation's top college football player each year.

That's an impressive legacy in community service. Though Martin's call to benevolence has been on track for many years, he recalls a significant news item from nearly two decades ago that inspired the formation of MAN Etc. Inc.

"One day I woke up and had this epiphany," Martin remembers. "It was formulated on the basis of the Central Park Jogger incident in 1989. You may recall that four African-American youths allegedly attacked a female jogger in Central Park. We were so appalled as African-American males that the incident happened that we started a program to go into the inner city and not only preach about how youth there can overcome that cycle but also to provide scholarships for them. Over the years we've raised literally hundreds of thousands of dollars each year. We're coming up on our twentieth anniversary, and we're proud of that. Those are athletes themselves going back into the communities and preaching that there's a formula for success. Frankly, I think it's better that you have an impact in the field of life than on the field of play."

The recognition of Martin's big heart doesn't end there. During the Journey for 9/11 walk itself, honors are bestowed on him wherever he goes, and Martin will tell you that all of them are extremely meaningful. Imagine being invited to Capitol Hill by a group of congressmen and women to introduce 9/11 legislation.

"They did it around my participation, which was a tremendous honor," says Martin, who also was recognized as a Person of the Week by ABC News and Charles Gibson. "That can only happen fifty-two times a year," he says of the network's recognition. Of the Heisman Humanitarian Award, Martin is humbled to be associated with the venerable industry name. "When you talk about superlatives," he says, "the word *Heisman* stands alone." Martin is the second recipient of the humanitarian award. "You talk about high points, they just continue to flow," he says. "We didn't do the walk for that reason, but those honors are just some of the fruits of our labor. And I use the plural term, because this is a group effort. It really is."

The fifty-mile day

As the Journey for 9/11 team closes in on a major milestone —completing one-third of the incredible cross-country trek, I

wondered if they now had a different appreciation of the magnitude of the task they'd undertaken, as opposed to when the walk
was merely an idea. We've all heard the axiom: Sometimes it's better not to know in advance what you're about to undertake, or
you might never start.

"I think if he knew some of the pitfalls we've encountered, he
would've just started walking," says Dianne.

"There's too much business around it," adds Reeves. "But if I
had known the physical [aspects], I don't know if I would have
signed on beforehand. Right now it's a pride thing. And she'll tell
you," he says, pointing at Dianne, "that George and I have a
$5,000 bet. I bet him five grand—and the five grand in any case
goes to Journey. The pledge is in my mom's name on the Web site,
and the deal is that if I leave this journey before it's over, I've got
to pay that five grand. If I survive the entire Journey—he can't run
me off, by the way—then *he's* got to pay the five grand. Either way,
the Journey gets five grand. Man, you just can't wrap your mind
around that, of what that means; that I'm going to walk from New
York to San Francisco."

George, however, takes a different view. From his perspective,
the trek has been a dream come true. But the dream was always
based on diligent preparation and sound attention to detail.

"Actually, I'd have to say that this has played out precisely," says
Martin. "You know when you go over something so much in your
mind, over and over again, even to the smallest detail, and you
know that certain elements of the country are going to be an
encounter that you've dreamed about? This has been running pretty
true to form. That's why I think it's a journey of destiny as much as
it is about the cause of the 9/11 [first responders]. I've been pleasantly surprised at how overwhelmingly positive it's been. There has
been virtually no negativity associated with it, on any front. That's
been the pleasant surprise."

One goal still remains out there, just beyond arm's reach. It is the subject of an ongoing discussion between Martin and Reeves, of which the latter speaks with respect and even a touch of reverence.

"What we're looking for is that flat surface so we can get a fifty-mile day in," says Reeves, with relish. "I don't think either of us really articulated that, but in the back of our minds that's that far-reaching goal we both have, to get in that fifty-mile day."

The vast reaches west of the Ozarks, extending across the Great Plains through the Texas Panhandle and then into eastern New Mexico, might well give them a shot at it. It'll be flat as a pancake.

"I'm telling you, we're hoping," Reeves says, "we both are waiting until we can hit that fifty-mile day. You can tell from talking to him that his heart is in it. He's not talking the talk, he is literally and figuratively walking the walk."

&8&8 &8&8 &8&8

As we leave the photo-op area where we had engaged Patra Minocha, Reeves looks through the front window and laughs. "Now, you see how much ground he's made since we left?"

It was true. The vehicle had rounded several curves and bends before finally catching up to Martin, who had pounded more than a mile down the road. We passed him and went on to where I had originally parked my car early in the afternoon.

But I pondered for a moment what Lee had said earlier: that if George stopped and made himself available to everyone he met, time-wise, they'd never get to California.

In those moments, as experienced that day, it is Reeves who tarries, informing interested people about the Journey and then handing them a brochure with the very important donation card, all the while listening to their concerns and fielding their comments, along with the praise, best wishes, and encouragement offered everywhere. Sometimes, as with the anti-terrorist, it's a little something more.

Chapter Six

EASE ON DOWN THE ROAD

While Martin hoofs westward, several major sporting events attract his interest. As the Daytona 500, the "Super Bowl of Stock Car Racing," was cranking up in Florida in mid-February, Martin was among several celebrities asked to predict the winner of the 2008 event.

"Dale Jarrett will take the checkered flag at the fiftieth running of the Great American Race, for two reasons," Martin prognosticated for www.finallapradio.com. "First, Dale is strong on superspeedways, and he will win the first NASCAR Sprint Cup Series race for Toyota. Second, his sponsor is UPS, which also supports A Journey for 9/11, my walk across the country."

Ultimate race winner Ryan Newman could make a strong case that Martin is no crystal-ball gazer. However, two weeks earlier, Martin had fared better with a sporting event closer to home: the Super Bowl.

"It was almost as indescribable as when *we* won the Super Bowl," says Martin from the Texas Panhandle of his own experience

George strikes a pose along the road overlooking Lake Maumelle, west of Little Rock, Arkansas.

as a member of the Giants' first Super Bowl champion team that capped the 1986 season. "It was a wonderful déjà vu. It was great to be such an integral part of it. Even though I wasn't in a Giants uniform, I'm part of the Giants family. Just to experience the anxiety that they went through, the doubters that had already proclaimed their opponent champions, and the insurmountable task that they had ahead of them, to see them all jell and stick together as a unit . . . I've got to tell you, sitting in the stands watching the game, I had as much butterflies and certainly as much elation as those guys had. Victory in Super Bowl Forty-two—that was the best feeling I've had in recent memory."

Incredibly, Martin had picked the Giants to win by three points, their actual margin of victory over the Patriots. "New England played right into the Giants' strength," he says of New York's big 17–14 win. "The Giants have an outstanding defense, as the Patriots have a good offense. But I thought that the Giants had a better team on defense than the Patriots had on offense; they were peaking at the right time."

With the Journey's adjusted route and timetable now projecting Martin to arrive in San Diego, the new termination point, on June 21, it isn't too far out to ask what his immediate plans include after the walk is finally completed.

"I think that's a misuse of the term *immediate*," Martin replies with a laugh. "The way Lee's projections are taking us, it won't be anytime immediate. But no, we really haven't made any concrete plans. We've talked about just the elation and the sense of gratification we're going to get when we can present the checks to the hospital on behalf of 9/11. We haven't really talked beyond that."

Actually, three hospitals will benefit: Hackensack University Medical Center in New Jersey, Mt. Sinai Medical Center, and North Shore Long Island Jewish Health Systems, the latter two New York-area hospital chains. All are Journey team sponsors.

People who complete a grand mission often can experience a letdown of sorts afterward, as the wildly pulsing energy from a sustained effort is suddenly replaced by an empty feeling, much like an elevator in free fall. Women birthing children know this well. Medically, they have a name for it: postpartum depression, the "baby blues." I wonder if Martin may be a candidate for that.

"You must be trying to get me divorced," he says, with a chuckle, "because the last thing my wife would ever want to hear out of my mouth is, 'Here's the next challenge.' Oh, I'm gonna keep that one to myself."

It is mentioned that former world heavyweight boxing champion George Foreman was reportedly interested in making yet another comeback sometime after he had retired from his *second* comeback, but that his wife stepped in and made her feelings known.

"She put the kibosh on that one?" Martin asks.

I told him I'd heard it was true. All men, I believe, sense their place in a relationship, instinctively knowing just how far they can take an idea before meeting resistance. I suspect Martin's wife, Dianne, has been a source of tremendous strength and support all their lives.

"When you look at it—and the answer is obviously affirmative—this is a young lady who has withstood high school sweetheart, college career, fourteen years in the NFL, and now almost twenty years in corporate America," Martin says, with genuine appreciation. "We've got thirty-five years invested in our relationship. We've got four wonderful children. We've got a family legacy and unity that, in an African-American community, although it's not unique, is not necessarily the norm. And we're very proud of that."

Martin pauses while continuing the pace. "Yeah, she has been the voice of reason behind this man," he says. "There have been a lot of things that haven't come to the light of day only because she says, 'Honey, don't be an idiot.' They say behind every great man there is a woman usually telling him what he's about to do is wrong."

"I think we used to first hear that about Nancy Reagan."

"Yes, exactly, right."

"We'd always hear how she was the brains behind her husband."

"Yes," Martin adds, "she's whispering in his ear, 'Honey, I don't think you want to do that.'"

Ides of March in the Texas Panhandle

Nearly four months after originally covering the Journey for 9/11 team in its traverse of central Tennessee, I catch up via phone with George and Lee, who are trekking through the Texas Panhandle, approaching a hamlet called Kress.

In early February, George and Company had been honored in Oklahoma City, Oklahoma, a "sister city" to New York City, says Reeves. It was from the Oklahoma capital that Gotham received unexpected but welcome help in the aftermath of 9/11. You could say that it takes one to know one, Oklahoma City having endured its own terrible tragedy in 1995, when the terrorist bombing of the

Alfred P. Murrah Federal Building killed 168 people and injured more than 800. But the seat of Oklahoma is a city that doesn't forget. Quick to respond to the 9/11 attacks, city officials sent manpower to assist Manhattan that infamous day when the twin towers of the World Trade Center fell in a heap. Oklahoma City honored Martin on February 11, 2008.

In a good-news continuation of America on its best behavior, which had evoked euphoria among the team during its travels through the Southeast, the Journey for 9/11 crew still had encountered no ugliness or unpleasantness due to race. It is a triumph for Americans, in light of the misperception by many that racism permeates our country's fabric to the core.

"Heading toward the New Mexico state line as we speak," says Reeves via phone in early March, "not one *single* incident. We've walked through areas where they'd never *seen* a black face, and we couldn't have been treated any more nicely or more hospitable. It's

COURTESY OF A JOURNEY FOR 9/11

Martin greets Oklahoma City police officers at the memorial for victims of the 1995 terrorist bombing of the Alfred P. Murrah Federal Building there.

been absolutely *un*believable. People treat us like royalty. They're not just cordial, they treat us like royalty."

And the fifty-mile day, that consummate quest for both George and Lee, still lies out there, like the Sirens hailing from the horizon, beckoning them to log the ultimate walking day. "No, not even close," admits Reeves, as the team neared its 2,000th mile. "Thirty is the record," he says of the pace set on November 19 outside Cookeville, Tennessee, and matched several times since.

Asked if the stick carried by Reeves for protection has ever been put to use, he replies, "Oh, absolutely, though we use the car more as a defensive mechanism than the stick." But where they are walking, wildlife is not incidental. Reeves recounts that they've journeyed onto dirt roads in the desolate Texas Panhandle and come across all manor of wildlife, from boar to deer to turkeys, and even a set of mountain lion paw prints. With dogs, the most common obstacle, several deterrents have proven effective.

"We've used the vehicle to block dogs, we've used the sticks to deter dogs, and we also have a taser," says Reeves. "What we've found is that just the sound of the taser is enough to deter ninety percent of the dogs that come our way."

As you might expect, Martin has worked his way through a bunch of walking shoes—nineteen, as of the Ides of March, as he closed in on his 2,000th mile. That's an average of about one pair for every 105 miles. By comparison, Reeves had walked almost eleven hundred miles of the same route and was only on his second pair.

"The difference is," Reeves says with a chuckle, "he is 250 *pounds* pounding that pavement every day."

I wonder out loud if there had been any other parts of the route since the 40 Bridge in Maryland that they were physically unable to walk. There was only one other place, somewhere in central Tennessee, Reeves recalls, that offered resistance—a stretch of just 120 feet! A bridge was out and the water below it was three feet deep. A welder at the site documented the impassibility of the span for the crew and mentioned that the bridge would be out for another month.

In a personal development, Reeves started out a single man at the George Washington Bridge last September but will be married by the trek's conclusion in impressive fashion. "We're going to tie the knot and do the nuptials on the USS *Midway* on the San Diego Embarcadero waterfront," he says. "The end of one journey, the beginning of another."

Along the way, Reeves proposed to his fiancée, Flor DeJesus, and that, also was in impressive fashion. In mid-December, with the Journey team in Bruceton, Tennessee, having completed its 1,000th mile not long before in Sawyer's Mill, Reeves flew in family members to the tiny hamlet. The crew gathered around the courthouse with the town mayor and other dignitaries for some pictures, with DeJesus operating the camera. According to Reeves, "She had that deer-in-the-headlights look on her face" about seeing so much family gathered, but she reasoned it away as a reunion of sorts, since Reeves's hometown of Jackson, Tennessee, was less than fifty miles away. They had gathered, all right, but not for that reason. With Bruceton civic officials and family looking on, Reeves dropped to one knee and pulled out a ring for Flor.

An interesting possibility has surfaced as the result of donations of hundreds of artifacts, gifts, and treasures by people along the Journey route. "We're thinking about a museum," says Reeves. "We're thinking about putting a museum in George's home, with all the things we've received since we've been on the road. We met one man who had a collection of Indian arrowheads. He had five thousand in his collection at one time. Interesting story: His son owns a restaurant called B. J.'s Burger Barn in Spiro, Oklahoma. George and I were walking by it one day in mid- to late January, but we didn't plan to stop there to eat. Then the owner comes out and introduces himself, and we wind up going back there for lunch. It was some of the best food we tasted on the entire trip!

"The man and his family have since become great friends of the Journey. They traveled with us to Oklahoma City and several other places just to participate in some of the events we had going on. His father, seventy-nine, is the one who collected the Indian arrowheads. Though most of his collection got stolen, he still had a few left, and he presented George with one of them at the Oklahoma City Memorial."

That's how mere acquaintances become good friends of the Journey team along the way. In another instance, an Oklahoma state trooper accompanied Martin across the Arkansas-Oklahoma line and walked some with George through the state before checking his available vacation days and blocking out time so he could reconnect with the team at the Oklahoma-Texas border. The officer also gave Martin some Oklahoma coins.

"George has got a collection of memorabilia from the road that is just impressive," says Reeves.

And a wealth of fond memories, too. A final one for this book is indicative of the wonderful occurrences that happen daily, according to Reeves. After meeting several well-wishers and curiosity seekers one morning, the team members were having lunch, when a man pulled up and said he'd been driving for hours looking for them. He indicated that the students and faculty of a school across the street from where they were eating had learned that the Journey for 9/11 team was passing through the area and had sent the man out to find them. He said he was returning to the school to tell them he couldn't find Martin and the Journey team when suddenly there they were.

"So when we started back out walking," says Reeves, "the school principal drove the school bus out with her student *council* and found us on the side of the road. I mean every *day* is like that." Unabashed amazement came out of my end of the phone. We both chuckled, and Lee let out a long breath.

"If I get *Alzheimer's*, I'll never forget this trip. Every day is a gift," he says.

※ ※ ※

The Journey for 9/11 team's dedication to task and its trench-level toughness are evident as each mile traveled leads to the next mile, and the next, and the hundreds after that. In the end, I'm just one more person who has slowed George down. But I don't think he'd look at it that way, not with regard to me or the thousands of other people he and Lee and the team have met along the way in one of the most unique opportunities a person will ever have to walk among his brethren. When I think of the literally tens of thousands of memories that George Martin and the Journey for 9/11 team are gathering on this trek, it is literally staggering.

To walk a portion, even a small one, of this transcontinental journey alongside a man like George Martin is to grasp the enormity of the quest as well as America. It's getting sore feet after a modest number of miles and then imagining Martin forging ahead, day after day, week after week, month after month, undefeatable.

An analogy drawn from his playing days with the Giants seems appropriate: In the end, the warrior stands victorious—muddied, bloodied, but unbowed.

PART TWO

TONY DUNGY

Staying the Course

Chapter Seven

"HE IS NOT AN ORDINARY MAN"

*T*he stillness of a winter night, just three days before Christmas, is shattered by the ringing telephone. It is 1:45 a.m. A groggy Lauren Dungy, the wife of Indianapolis Colts head coach Tony Dungy, picks up the phone and hands it to her husband. It isn't unusual for Dungy to get a middle-of-the-night phone call. Typically, it is one of his players who has stepped off the path, perhaps gotten into some sort of altercation, run afoul of the law, or has a more desperate problem that requires the assistance of his mentor and coach. I hope one of our guys isn't hurt, Dungy thinks, as he wonders what kind of news awaits him on the other end of the line.

It couldn't have been worse. It's the call every parent dreads.

A nurse at a local Tampa, Florida, hospital tells Dungy their eighteen-year-old son, Jamie, is dead. It appears he has taken his own life.

Immediately, as an instinctive action, Dungy begins to pray. But the horrible news is too overwhelming to shut out and is already seeping into his not-yet-fully-awake consciousness. It is too late, in this instance, even for prayer.

∞∞ ∞∞ ∞∞

As Dungy relates in his book *Quiet Strength: The Principles, Practices, and Priorities of a Winning Life,* the next several days "were all a fog." So many questions, so few answers. Jamie had been well liked; he was a handsome, compassionate, caring kid. To Dungy, his oldest son had been so like his mother, gentle and sensitive, the kind of child that was helpful and kind to kids who were picked on.

Fortunately, friends can provide an invaluable aid, almost a shield, at times of paralyzing shock. People who knew the Dungys flocked from all over the country to help the stricken family. Complicating the funeral arrangements was the fact that it was now three days before Christmas, and on top of that the Colts had a game in two days—on Christmas Eve, at Seattle. Obviously, the game had been eclipsed by the enormity of the Dungys' loss, and Indianapolis team President Bill Polian announced that assistant head coach Jim Caldwell would take over as interim boss on the sidelines.

In the Dungys' hometown of Tampa, the funeral loomed.

∞∞ ∞∞ ∞∞

As the successful head coach of the Tampa Bay Buccaneers from 1996-2001, Dungy had made many friends in the Big Guava. He had taken a downtrodden team that hadn't logged a winning season since 1982 and guided it to a second-place finish in the NFC's tough Central Division in 1997. Two years later, he brought the Bucs to the NFC Championship Game. But expectations eventually exceeded reality. When Tampa Bay incurred two blowout playoff losses the next two seasons (2000-01), Dungy was canned. His family, however, had found a welcome home in Tampa and, even after being named as the Colts' head coach only a week after being let go by the Buccaneers, he and Lauren elected to maintain their primary residence there. One of the deep area friendships Dungy had formed was with Abe Brown.

Brown had started a prison ministry back in 1976, when one of his former players—Brown was a longtime coach at Tampa's Blake High School—wound up behind bars. Twenty-one years later, when Dungy came to town, Brown had asked the Bucs' newly installed head coach if he wanted to visit some prisons with him. Dungy said okay and accompanied Brown on a trip to the Polk Correctional Institution in Polk City northeast of Tampa. It was a "take," as they say in Hollywood.

"I recall vividly the first time he offered to go with us," says the eighty-one-year-old Brown of Dungy's inaugural prison visit in 1997. "It was a pleasant surprise. I knew it would be refreshing for the men, but I didn't realize what an impact it would make on Coach Dungy. Having been a football coach and having dealt with young men for a good part of my life, I knew what his presence and his interest meant and what good could come out of a man of his stature taking time out to come and see losers and get his life involved—to put interest in life's losers in order for them to become winners in life. Of course the warden and all of the officers were pleased that Coach Dungy would take time out and come to the prison. The problem they had then was who was going to come and who couldn't come. You couldn't get them all in an audience at the same time."

Dungy had made a connection, his personable demeanor immediately touching the inmates. "The men just absolutely fell in love with him," says Brown. "He didn't just talk at them, he talked *to* them. He gave them the opportunity to ask questions and was very cautious about not overlooking anybody, about not being in a hurry. He took the time to answer any questions that anybody would ask. Then, of course, when we finished that engagement, practically every prison in the state of Florida made a request for him to come there also. Now we get calls from wardens all over the state begging us to put them on his schedule. But then, we have such a limited time we just do the very best that we can."

Yes, a top NFL head coach only has so much time away from the ball, even for causes as worthwhile as Brown's prison visitations. "He didn't have but a few opportunities that he could take out from his busy schedule and go into the prison," Brown recalls. "The question then was what prison was going to be the lucky one in order for it to have Coach Dungy come and speak. He has been well received in the state of Florida, and of course now he is well received throughout the nation."

Brown, like almost everyone who comes into contact with the mild-mannered Colts coach, is struck by the uncommon depth of Dungy as a human being.

"He is a Godly man," says Brown without reservation. "It is difficult to find men who are successful in athletics and make the kind of money that people do in athletics and still remain on a common basis, taking time out to deal with the less fortunate.

"Some of us have said we are Christians, but we have not actually lived the Christian life," Brown continues. "The Christian life is a life of giving, not receiving. When a person has a giving nature, it comes off loud and clear. When they are talking with people, they can't help but project the fact that they're a giver. It is not a burden for them to be in a place, such as a prison, to talk to losers. That comes off in a number of ways, and the men perceive that. So without saying so, actions, we've been taught, speak louder than words. The men read that, and they certainly appreciate it.

"It is almost unbelievable to see the response of the officers, inmates, and everybody concerned when Tony Dungy comes into a prison. We have the largest federal prison in the country here in Florida, and we have gone into the federal prison a couple of times. He is not in a hurry; he takes his time to sign autographs. He spends as much time as they will allow him. It has been a real remarkable experience."

For prison inmates as well as officials, Brown likens the occasions of a Dungy visit to the excitement accompanying a favorite holiday. "I can tell you that on the day that Tony Dungy is coming into the prison, it is like Christmas Day," Brown says. "Brightness is all over the institution. They put on another face and they forget about where they are and who they are. It is just a different atmosphere altogether. I can sense it. I have never seen anybody else that comes into a prison have quite that same effect, and I've been going into them now for thirty years or more."

Brown imparted one last comment about the gift of prison ministry, a reflection that sheds a most admirable light on the Colts' head coach. "You know, the Bible teaches that Christ styled himself as a prisoner. 'I was in prison, I was naked, I was a stranger and you came not unto me, but when you do it unto the least of these, you do it also unto me.'"

Then, with the humility of a true servant, Brown adds: "He is not an ordinary man. I am not in the class that Tony Dungy is in, but we both serve the same Captain."

Attentive parents

This ability to stand so tall in the world's eyes yet be one with people of lesser opportunity stems from a belief far greater than mere praiseworthy words. This exceptional quality has forged the inner, quiet strength of Tony Dungy. It is a core faith that winds back to his childhood in Jackson, Michigan, where he grew up as the second oldest in a family of four under the attentive parenting of a mother and father who were both college graduates, teachers, and possessed advanced degrees from Michigan State. Mother CleoMae, who taught high school English, earned a master of arts in English, while father Wilbur, a physiology professor and one of the first African-American teachers in Michigan's community college system, held a doctorate in physiology. But most of all, Dungy and his siblings benefited from belonging to an intact family centered on a strong belief in God and a deep, abiding respect for others.

"I feel like that has been a blessing," notes Dungy of his youth. "You don't get to pick your parents and your relatives. I did have that support system. I had a two-parent home—both parents that really cared about you and were there all the time and had that background of education that they stressed. It was fantastic for all four of us."

Both parents guided their children through example. The late CleoMae Dungy, born in Ontario, Canada, was a top athlete, playing on Canadian junior basketball teams in her youth. Though she passed away in 2002 from complications arising from diabetes, much of the athleticism found in the family is credited to her. Dr. Wil Dungy, who boxed and participated in track and field in his youth, professed a strong belief as an adult that team sports existed to help provide critical life lessons for kids.

One of the more tangible illustrations of Wil Dungy's admirable traits of patience and calm character surfaced on a fishing expedition in the summer of 1965, an occasion on which he took along sons Tony, then nine years old, and Linden, age five. The elder Dungy was teaching his boys how to cast, when he calmly asked Linden to stop what he was doing and not move. Tony noticed his father's hand slowly move to his ear and, while calmly reminding Linden to always look behind as well as ahead before casting, worked Linden's hook free from his ear without flinching.

"I learned something that day," noted Dungy, who couldn't help but admire his father's patience and calmness under fire.

In addition to academia, Dungy's father further distinguished himself as one of the famed Tuskegee Airmen—the U.S. Army Air Corps' legendary experimental training ground for black pilots and support personnel during World War II—a fact completely unknown to Tony until his father passed away in 2004.

"That was just my dad's way, and he did some awesome things," says Dungy. "You know, he could have certainly bragged about a lot of things, but he never really did. He was a very, very humble person, and even my coaches and friends that were around him for a long time didn't know a lot of the things he did. As a family, I think we found out about the Tuskegee Airmen from a friend of his at the funeral."

All of this resulted in a grounded, nurtured upbringing for a young African-American boy. And at its core stood the one element that has made Dungy the man he is today.

"It's hard to overestimate the importance of the lessons my parents taught me," Dungy acknowledges. "However, there is one gift they bestowed that I would place above all others: faith."

That faith was rooted in not only Dungy's parents but his grandparents as well. His paternal grandfather had been a minister, occasionally teaching at Detroit Bible College. From his mother's side of the family, he received plenty of what he calls "godly heritage," plus his mother was a Sunday school teacher. The sum of it all imprinted Dungy at an early age.

"I was around it and heard it my whole life and understood that accepting Christ meant going to heaven," says Dungy about his early introduction to religion. "I understood that part of it probably from the time I was three or four years old. My mom was a Sunday school teacher. Wednesday or Thursday nights, she would practice her lessons on us and tell us Bible stories. I knew those stories before I could even read or write."

Young athlete, young coach

Bolstered by this substantial armor of deep religious belief, Dungy set out into a world he found himself easily attracted to as a boy: athletics. Not surprisingly, for a kid slightly built, Dungy embraced basketball early on, but his skill at football quickly became evident at Frost Junior High School in Jackson. In December 2006, a blogger posted an interesting account of the young Dungy on Yahoo! Sports' "NFL Rumors" that revealed future coaching potential in the young athlete.

"Our East Jackson eighth-grade football team played against Tony Dungy," says blogger d9a2v4 of a game in 1968. "He was a man amongst boys even then. He was known to 'coach' opposing players after games and scrimmages, giving tips on quarterbacking techniques."

Several years later, at Parkside High School, Dungy started and starred at quarterback in his sophomore and junior years. Then, an impulsive action almost derailed his promising athletic career. As a captain-elect of the football team his senior year, Dungy quit the squad in protest over what he perceived to be a race-related slight: a talented black teammate whom Dungy felt deserved to be named co-captain alongside him was snubbed. A boycott by the team's black players ensued. It was then that the first major mentor outside his family appeared in Dungy's life.

Into the gap stepped Leroy Rocquemore, an African-American junior high school administrator whom Dungy had first met while a student at Frost Junior High. The mild-mannered Rocquemore negotiated a peace between Dungy and his discipline-minded football coach, continually driving home the point that, thirty years from then, Dungy could very possibly harbor a deep regret at having passed up a onetime opportunity to experience the fun of being a captain and a senior playing his final year of high school football—no matter what the initial cause for his unhappiness.

The incident figures prominently in Dungy's unfolding. Had he not played football his senior year—Dungy at the time felt his future lay in basketball—he in all likelihood would not have played college football or continued into the NFL as a player. As for coaching a future Super Bowl champion? Not very probable.

"I see now what I couldn't as a strong-willed teenager," Dungy admits today. "If Mr. Rocquemore hadn't taken that interest in me, everything would've been different.

But history records that Rocquemore did intervene, and Dungy found himself being courted by a number of universities. Minnesota, with Cal Stoll as head coach, made the most attractive offer: Dungy would be allowed to play both football and basketball. The youngster wound up earning gridiron honors as a two-time team MVP, placing fourth all-time in Big Ten total offense, and being selected captain of the Golden Gophers his senior season. There were a couple of other notables that Dungy took with him from college: revulsion for neckties (gained from office-type summer employment) and a huge afro.

"I looked as if I had just walked off the stage from a Sly and the Family Stone gig," he once said.

Chapter Eight

UNDER A
MENTOR'S WING

Tony Dungy was not selected in the 1977 NFL Draft, a nonevent that "crushed" him. While the Canadian Football League's Montreal Alouettes offered $50,000 for him to sign, NFL teams were proffering bonuses in the $1,000 to $5,000 range. It seemed the last place on earth that would make sense for a newcomer to play professional football was Pittsburgh.

That was during the middle of the Steelers' dynasty years, and the club was stocked with *eleven* Pro Bowl players. A good report from Tom Moore, his position coach at Minnesota who had just been hired by Pittsburgh, informed the organization and head coach Chuck Noll in particular that Dungy was a smart player who could fit in somewhere for them. The club offered him a $2,200 signing bonus and a salary of $20,000 if he made the final roster. Dungy signed and became a Steeler.

"I just never looked at it as a coincidence," he says. "At the time I was hurt that I wasn't drafted and thought I should have been. I still don't know why I made a decision to go to Pittsburgh. It really affected my whole life and my whole career from then on out. Looking back on it, it wasn't really a logical decision, and I usually pride myself on being very logical and doing the wise thing. I don't know what to say about that, other than I really think it was just the Lord's will."

Though Dungy's NFL career as a defensive back spanned a modest four seasons with three teams, two invaluable years were with Pittsburgh, including the Super Bowl XIII championship year of 1978. Brief though his stay was in the NFL as a player, he managed to log his fifteen minutes of fame—or infamy, depending on how you look at it. Dungy is the last player in NFL history to have made an interception and thrown an interception in the same game. It occurred during a 27–10 loss at Houston on October 9, 1977, when, in addition to his regular play at safety, he wound up under center in the fourth quarter after starting quarterback Terry Bradshaw and backup Mike Kruczek went out with injuries.

More importantly, though, Dungy was exposed to a superb team and the thoughtful, supportive process of a winning coach. Both furthered his Christian beliefs and expanded his humanity.

"It wasn't until later on that I really understood that how you lived and what you did was so important, and that we did have a purpose to be on Earth and it wasn't necessarily just to go to school and to win games," says Dungy. "It was really to honor God with whatever we chose to do, and that probably didn't hit me until I was probably twenty-one years old, as a young player with the Steelers, when I was around so many more mature Christian athletes. Looking back on it, I know the Lord led me there to really put me with those guys who could really be that mentoring system that I needed."

He credits a pack of former teammates with shoring up his faith, most notably safety Donnie Shell—"one of the most fired-up Christians I ever met"—who would chide the young Dungy for his lack of faith during tough times. Dungy looks back at that time as a key period of development with his faith. A bout with mononucleosis prior to the start of training camp in 1978 had sidelined Dungy, and being a reserve on a team loaded with future Hall of Famers and all-stars, he naturally began to worry about his place on the squad, second-guessing his decision to sign with Pittsburgh as a free agent after college. Sensing that Dungy was putting football first, ahead of God, Shell confronted the young player in that walk-the-walk way that many devout Christians employ in their faith.

"I think that was the point at which I really began to understand what it means to be a Christian," Dungy said of his time under Shell's tutelage. "It was the first time I was able to look at football as something that God was allowing me to do, not something that should define me."

Perhaps the person who first illuminated for Dungy the potential benefits of coaching football players in a humane way was his first professional mentor, Chuck Noll, the Steelers' highly respected field boss and an enshrinee in the Pro Football Hall of Fame in Canton, Ohio. The fabled Pittsburgh coach was a tough taskmaster but eminently fair.

"I was really fortunate to play for Coach Noll," recalls Dungy. "When I got to Pittsburgh, I had never played defense at all; a little bit in junior high, but none in high school and college. So now I had come to professional football, and I am out there making elementary mistakes that are costing the professional football players games, very critical mistakes that I should have known. But Coach Noll, when I would come to the sideline, would say, 'Now tell me, explain to me what you were thinking there. What were you looking at? Why do you think this mistake happened?'

"It helped me grow. That's when I understood that's what I needed as a coach, and that's what got me to be a better player—not somebody saying, 'That's the dumbest mistake! How could you do that? Any novice would know that!' He just didn't approach it that way. So I saw it on two levels—from my parents and from

Coach Noll—how to really be constructive and get people to play as well as they can play."

A mature knack for motivating players through a sense of purpose rather than the time-honored technique of intimidation through fear was one of the commendable characteristics about Noll.

"Coach Noll always told me that players want to be good and that it's the coach's job to teach them and give them the tools they need to improve," says Dungy. "I never have been the type to get in people's face, and I never will be. I think at first my approach catches some guys by surprise, because they may have heard the intimidation-through-fear routine time and time again, from high school all the way through college.

"But that's how Coach Noll was with us. He always said you've got to prepare for your life's work. 'We are going to work hard; it is a tough job that you have out here on the field, but it is only preparing you for other things,' and that's what I try to get across to my players. 'Yes, we are going to do everything we can to win, but we are not going to let it pervade our whole life and our whole personality, and we are going to try to make sure we have time to do other things. We are going to take time off when we get to Super Bowl week. Yes, we could go down on Sunday, but we're going to spend that weekend with our families. We'll have plenty of time to prepare for the Bears later.' I think once the players understand that it's okay, they enjoy it, they like the concept. But for some of them, it is different and it's hard for them to grasp it at first."

The Colts' main man is, nevertheless, still surprised at the responses he receives from players unfamiliar with his humane dictum that places the family at the top of the priority list.

"It is striking to me," he continues. "When I talk to my players in the first meeting, I'll say, 'Now, you have to understand: Family situations always come first. If you have any type of crisis, any type of problem family-wise, all you need to do is tell me what it is and go take care of it.' Invariably, in the course of the year, I will have guys say, 'My wife is going in to have surgery. I just don't know how to ask you this, but can I miss practice?' And I have to say, 'You know we have already discussed this.' It's just so different for them that they are still not quite certain until they have been around a while, and then they really understand."

Dungy's family-first premise has been subjected to some severe testing. The night before Indianapolis's big 2005 AFC Divisional Playoff tilt with eventual Super Bowl champion Pittsburgh, then-Colts safety Nick Harper was knifed in the thigh by his girlfriend during a domestic dispute. Besides the obvious health-related concern for his player, there was also the very real possibility that the event would become a blown-out-of-proportion distraction at this critical juncture for his team. Dungy was asked if he had become involved in the Harper incident, but his response indicates that he didn't place it above any other player-related matters. His appreciation is clear, though, that the Colts organization has his back.

"We have had a lot of those [incidents like Harper's], and you just have to really be there," the Indy mentor says. "I think all of my players understand they can come in and they can talk to anybody on our staff about that. We have a support group specifically for those things, and it is just something the Colts, starting with Mr. [Jim] Irsay, really believe in."

Interacting with players in times of personal crisis is nothing new to the league or its personnel. Not a coach in the land—college or pro—is exempt from players' issues landing in their lap. But whom would you rather take your problems to, a square-jawed boot-camp D.I. or the sensitively in-tune Dungy?

And Brown begat Noll who begat Dungy

Through all phases of the Colts coach's unfolding legacy, a historic lineage runs, a heritage if you will, that understandably stirs his pride.

"Chuck Noll developed much of his coaching philosophy from the legendary Paul Brown, and I got mine from Chuck," Dungy has noted. "I tell people that I'm from the Paul Brown school of football."

Noll, who guided his Steelers teams to four Super Bowl triumphs in the 1970s, presented a doctrine of coaching that stressed emphasis not only on what a player did between the chalk stripes, but also on that person's eventual life's work. In the coach's estimation, football was just something you did now to prepare for your ultimate purpose. He illustrated that clearly in his own life, believing that all facets of a person's life are equally important. Noll cooked, flew airplanes, drove boats, grew roses, was a history buff, and wasn't one to hang around the Steelers offices after work was completed—unlike a multitude of NFL coaches who are slaves to the job, putting in absurd hours at their craft to the exclusion of family.

Noll's example wasn't lost on Dungy, who today carries a distinct families-first attitude into his profession. That approach is considered a benchmark within the ranks of coaching, in that it was just forty years ago that the granite-like Vince Lombardi style—the "winning is everything" construct—ruled the league, establishing fear through in-your-face intimidation.

"I think we had, especially twenty years ago, a belief of what style was successful and what you had to look like to be a successful coach in the NFL," says Dungy today, entering his seventh season as head coach of the Indianapolis Colts, the 2006 world champions. "I think I battled that as much as anything else, to show people that I could do it this way and not have people believing that you're not going to be able to discipline these guys if you are not going to intimidate them; that you are not going to be able to be effective if you won't work those long hours and say that this is the only job that you are concerned about in your life. So, I think I am more proud of overcoming that and just showing people that what I believe in can work in any field, any endeavor, even in the NFL, where historically it hasn't been viewed that way."

In Dungy's scheme, the player is given an opportunity to embrace freedom within his system, which stresses personal responsibility and accountability. But just because there's no Vince Lombardi or Bill Parcells crawling around inside his skin, don't get the impression that Dungy runs a recreation center for his players.

"You are treated like a man," notes Indianapolis Colts center Jeff Saturday. "That is the part he expects you to be able to handle, the responsibility that you've been given as a member of the team and the profession we're in. He expects you to act like it. He gives you the opportunity to prove—not only to yourself but to him, the team, and the NFL as a whole—that you're man enough to handle this responsibility. He doesn't shortchange you.

"The one thing I have respected about his style of leadership is that he allows other people to lead. He gives them an opportunity to be leaders on his team, and he allows you to do it. To me, the only way teams can ever be really effective as a team is when the players take control and say, 'Hey this is ours, this is our team; we have to take responsibility for this.' He encourages that, and I think that is what has made us a successful team. I also think it has helped his coaching style, because he doesn't have to take everything on himself, he can give it to other people."

Not everyone has viewed Dungy's mild-mannered leadership approach with enthusiasm. In a celebrated incident during the off-season following the 2002 campaign, in which the Colts were rudely ousted from the playoffs in a 41–0 loss to the New York Jets, outspoken placekicker Mike Vanderjagt hurled barbs through the press at Dungy's even-keeled style of coaching, as well as teeing off on iconic quarterback Peyton Manning. Dungy was furious and prepared to can Vanderjagt, summoning the kicker from his home in Toronto for that purpose. But by the time Vanderjagt arrived in Indy, Dungy's then-sixteen-year-old son Jamie, who had befriended the kicker during the season, had talked his dad out of the dismissal.

"This is the way I coach," Dungy stated about the incident. "I believe it is the best way to win football games and lead people. I had grown up with that philosophy. My mom used to say that a good leader gets people to follow him because they want to, not because he makes them."

While Jamie Dungy did in fact prolong Vanderjagt's stay in Indianapolis—a move that benefited the Colts particularly during the 2003 season, when the kicker was perfect on thirty-seven field-goal attempts en route to an NFL-record forty-two consecutive field goals—ultimately he was let go, after failing badly in the clutch during the 2005 AFC playoffs. He signed with Dallas for 2006 but didn't last the season and is now out of the league.

Saturday, a three-time Pro Bowler, clearly experienced the difference in the Dungy method, having been a carryover from the Colts' previous coaching regime.

"Coach [Jim] Mora [Dungy's predecessor at Indy] gave me my first start, so I have a lot of great respect for him," says Saturday. "But his management was much different than Coach Dungy's. He had the mentality of putting guys on a disciplined program and running it that way. He was the guy who was going to keep everybody in line. When Coach Dungy came in, he was not a yeller at all. He was very quiet. The word I use to describe him all the time, kind of a biblical term, is *meek*. You know he just has this meekness about him, by definition, that quiet strength. He has it.

"He would list his rules, but instead of getting excited about them, he would just tell you, 'Hey, here are the rules that I expect you to follow.' He'd set them in front of the team and would say, 'If you can't follow my rules, it is not that I don't think you are a good football player or that I don't think you can be successful at other places, but this is what I know wins, and I won't take less than this.' That was a real distinct difference in the way I had seen people lead in the past. He never gets upset and yells at people. He really just tries to lay down the

From the wise to the warrior: Dungy gives Indianapolis quarterback Peyton Manning last-second advice before the start of another Colts drive.

boundaries, and then he lets you be as successful within those boundaries as you can be.

"I have a great deal of respect for the opportunity to play for a man like that," Saturday says. "I am a Christian as well, and to be able to follow a man like him and watch the way he patterns his life and lives his life—not only is it impressive, but it is something you can pattern yourself after, and that is always an encouragement."

Dungy sees his personal approach as part of a larger scheme, one he's grown into with a high level of comfort. "I really believe my leadership style is formed by my value system, which is definitely Christian," he acknowledges, "and so everything I do is going to be based on that. Part of the Christian walk is perseverance. It is believing what you stand for and being willing to continue to persevere."

Dungy's firm-but-fair philosophy was in evidence early in his head-coaching career, back during his first season with Tampa Bay, in 1996. "I was upset because two players had missed personal appearances," he recalled of separate incidents involving running back Errict Rhett, the former University of Florida Gators star, and that year's No. 1 draft pick, defensive end Regan Upshaw. At a morning meeting, Dungy addressed the team. He told them plainly that Rhett and Upshaw were "not the disease but merely symptoms of a bigger problem," saying he felt too many of the players held the belief that if something didn't benefit them personally, then it was unimportant.

"Champions know it's important," Dungy told his first Buccaneers team. "You have to understand that all the little things the coaches are asking of you really do matter. Knowing I can count on you is just as important to me as your talent. You'll always find excuses for not doing what you're supposed to do. But that's exactly what creates a losing environment."

Sounding like a man with the oratorical skills of William Jennings Bryan, Dungy as head coach sees no value in forcefully cramming his way down your throat. He gets to you because you can't hide from his logic and reason. On top of that, you know he's for real. He's almost too good to be true for an NFL head coach, at least in the traditional sense. Players from the 1950s might not have responded to someone like Dungy appealing to their better sides, looking to infuse them with motivation and inspiration as a result of their grasping a concept. Well, maybe everyone from that era but the Paul Brown-coached teams.

Dungy has said that the Tampa meeting in '96 was his biggest blowup in his entire head-coaching career. Can you imagine! Lombardi would have laughed. But then St. Vincent would be dumfounded at his own ineffectiveness today, his dictatorial ways for the most part falling on players' deaf ears.

The first year in Tampa Bay was not without its lessons, and the attentive Dungy was there to pick up on all of them. But the turn-around 1997 season, in which the Bucs shockingly reversed a horrid 6–10 record from the year before, ultimately coaxed Dungy into admitting, even after his Super Bowl triumph in 2006, that that magical season with the Buccaneers was his all-time favorite in football. The entire Tampa community came alive, charged with the current of the new Bucs success. Excitement hung in the air and people felt it. It would lead to a classic Dungy line: "I found that while life drags on when you're losing, it marches on when you're winning."

Dungy's philosophy was suffusing his players. Best of all, it was working. One of the truly refreshing elements of his belief system is the respectful way in which he approaches everything, which fairly flies in the face of traditional NFL head-coaching methodology.

"If we get caught up in chasing what the world defines as success," says Dungy, "we can use our time and talent to do some great things. We might even become famous. But in the end, what will it mean? What will people remember us for? Are other people's lives better because we lived? Did we make a difference? Did we use the fullest gifts and abilities God gave us? Did we give our best effort, and did we do it for the right reasons?"

For all the genuineness of his beliefs, Dungy is only too aware that, while "society tends to define success in terms of accomplishments, awards, material possessions, and profit margins, in the football business, winning is the only thing that matters."

Yet even against that unchallengeable edict, Dungy sticks to his guns about football's place in his life. "It's the journey that matters," he has said. "Learning is more important than the test. Practice well, and the games will take care of themselves. Football is just a game. It's not a way of life. It doesn't provide any sort of intrinsic meaning. It's just football. It lasts three hours, and when the game is over, it's over. Frankly, that fact—that when it's over, it's over—is part of football's biggest appeal to me. The coaches and players really don't have time to celebrate or to stay down, because Sunday's gone and Monday's here."

His understanding of the duality of "win, but win without sacrificing who you are" has honed Dungy into a mentor whose calm, direct demeanor influences virtually everyone he meets, impacting players, coaches, fans, and even team owners. And as you would imagine, a man of that quality wouldn't be happy just winning championships.

Chapter Nine

ALL PRO DAD

After Dungy's first season in Tampa, the Bucs' head coach hooked up with an area group called Family First. Two years later, he helped the organization cofound a new program called All Pro Dad, an assemblage that promotes strengthening families and making sure that dads step up to their most important mission: being a father. The organization had come across a stunning fact: two-thirds of African-American teens have absent fathers. Dungy, through his ministering with Abe Brown in prisons, heard inmates say that the most common factor among them was that there was no father in the home when they were growing up. Dungy felt that was enough information to begin to target dads for his group.

Dungy even held the mirror up to himself and wasn't very pleased with his critical assessment. What he saw was a man whose father spent more time with him than he was managing to do with his own children. The life of an NFL head coach is an all-consuming occupation, and even though Dungy was religious about making time for his family, he still felt he came up short in comparison with his own dad.

"It is definitely a cause that I feel a tremendous amount of passion about," says Dungy. "I try to do as much with my kids as I can. I certainly enjoy all the time I am able to spend with them. I have my kids at work a lot and do different projects with them. I think if I was grading myself, I would say I am probably a B-minus to a C-plus, whereas I thought my dad was an A, because he was around all the time and he just had much more time than I have. I think I use my time as well as I can, and I have learned a lot of creative things from All Pro Dad and from talking to other guys. But I just wish I had more time to be there [with the kids] and be around."

For many in the African-American community, a deluge of formidable elements seem to conspire to keep families apart. "It has just been amazing, the kind of society we have generated, with both parents having to work to keep the family going, the divorce rate," notes Dungy. "There are a lot things causing it and leading up to it, but the one thing Family First has found is that small things can make a big difference, even giving just a little significant time. If you are like I am, where you work and have times when you are going to be away two to three weeks because of a job commitment, or you know you are going to miss a certain amount of time, just doing the little things—phone calls, little notes, small things you can do, taking ten minutes—really helps out. They are very important."

"We're so blessed to have had ten years of good success, and we've got decades more to go," says All Pro Dad spokesman Darrin Gray, the program's public relations director. "There's something special going on here, not just in the NFL but around the country, where guys understand that 'character first' can now lead not only to on-the-field wins but can lead to community wins, community impact."

At the outset, the trio of Family First head Mark Merrill, Bucs (now Colts) receivers coach Clyde Christensen, and Dungy collectively brainstormed and prayed for direction for the fledgling program. It was decided to schedule an event for fathers and kids following a Tampa Bay Bucs training camp session. To their amazement, thousands descended upon the facility for the event.

"They kind of looked at themselves and said, 'We're on to something,'" says Gray. "Mark, over time, began to mobilize around that opportunity and figure out how to develop a curriculum, programming, and platforms to help communicate to dads across America. And when we say 'dads,' All Pro Dad is a brand that works well, but we're talking about mentors and grandfathers and uncles and teachers and educators and coaches—anyone who wants to take an active role in the life of a young person."

All Pro Dad utilizes Dungy and fifty-one other NFL athletes, coaches, and alumni to help move its message through a variety of channels, the most high-profile of which is All Pro Dad Father & Kids Experience, a large community event run in NFL facilities. Some of the higher-profile NFL players contributing their time and effort to the organization include Hall of Famers Steve Largent and Anthony Muñoz, as well as current stars Aaron Kampman, Jon Kitna, and Kyle Brady. Other head coaches in the league have committed to the cause, among them Herm Edwards (Kansas City) and Mike Tomlin (Pittsburgh).

"These are all high-character guys that Tony signs off on," says Gray. "These people have the same values that we do—faith, family, and football, in that order."

The organization uses the major events to promote All Pro Dad's Day chapters. "And if you've talked to Tony about where his heart's at," says Gray, "this is what he's most excited about. Big events are great—they generate a lot of publicity and we use those and work with media to move this message—but really, it comes down to getting these chapters started."

One of the people who helped pioneer the chapter concept is Pat Fitzgerald, a heating and air-conditioning company owner in

Indianapolis and an impassioned speaker for All Pro Dad, whom Gray finds inspiring. "As All Pro Dad was growing, we didn't know how all this would morph and what it would become," says Gray. "We just knew we were going to move this message and were going to find a way to make connections and serve men. Lo and behold, we found out that other organizations have chapter systems that work well, and we try to emulate those. We want to help dads tie relational knots with their kids. Pat was instrumental and involved in some of that early stage stuff."

Fitzgerald's story opens with a sad account about his own relationship with his father. Generally disappointing his father as a youth, Fitzgerald got the boot—not out of the house but out of his father's life—after young Pat was told that he was holding the family back.

"He was trying to shock me into realizing I was walking the wrong path," remembers Fitzgerald, age fifty-eight and the father

Coach Dungy talks to a rapt audience of dads and their children at an All Pro Dad Father & Kids Experience at the Colts' practice facility in Indianapolis.

of five, "but it didn't work for me. I remember him walking out of the room, and I threw my fist up in the air and went, 'Yahoooo! No more curfew!' It took me forty more years before I realized that I wish he had thrown me out of the house but kept me *in* his life."

In later years, his folks having moved to Florida, Fitzgerald became the dutiful son, visiting often. He challenged himself to get up the nerve to tell his father that he loved him, but it wasn't until the latter was approaching death that both managed to come forward with the healing phrase. In the interim, though, in fact throughout his lifetime, Fitzgerald began to understand, that much love actually had been directed his way by his dad, not in so many words but rather through actions.

"He was a traveling salesman and wasn't home during the week," says Fitzgerald, "but on the weekends he never missed any of our games when he was home. If we blew the baseball game, he'd take us to the Dog and Suds and get us root beers. It's kind of like he was saying that losing's part of life, just like winning. Celebrate those parts, too. All those things that he did that screamed 'I love you!' that I never realized. I needed to hear it in my heart first. It was just a wonderful thing."

Some years back, Fitzgerald's eldest daughter, then a senior in high school, involved him in her Christian Awakening weekend, in which the kids go away for four days and talk about themselves, friends, family, and God. In the process, parents are asked to write their child a letter. At the weekend's conclusion, the letters are read out loud in front of the other seniors, as are letters from the kids to their parents. Fitzgerald was profoundly affected. It became the basis for new, meaningful interaction with his children.

"The thing just smacked me right in the face," he says. "They want to know how much they've meant to you over the last eighteen years and how much you truly love them. It is just so powerful. The kids, maybe for the first time in their lives, realize the true love their parents have for them, even though the usual daily clutter gets in the way."

From those formative seeds of parent-child relating, Fitzgerald and an old Indianapolis friend, Bill Bissmeyer, began talking about their dads. Then Bill's teenage son, John, died suddenly of a rare heart disease, and Bissmeyer, in an attempt at forming an informal support group, suggested getting together with Fitzgerald and several other fathers and their children once a month for breakfast—a time during which everyone could casually share, connect, and further bond.

"We thought it would be me, Bill, and a couple of other guys," recalls Fitzgerald of those early Dad's Day breakfast get-togethers. The very first meeting drew fifteen people. The following month forty-five fathers and kids turned out. "Then the next month it was sixty-five, and the one after that eighty-five," Fitzgerald cites. "It spread here in Indiana pretty quickly."

From the beginning, Bissmeyer's Dad's Day breakfasts in Indiana were in no way connected with All Pro Dad. Of course, it was inevitable that the two would eventually hook up.

"All Pro Dad started with Tony down in Tampa," Fitzgerald recounts. "When Tony came to Indianapolis to coach the Colts, they were up here doing some PR work with Tony and heard about our organization, Dad's Day Breakfasts. So they called us. They wanted to know if we could sit down and talk about our breakfast program and see if it was something they could use. They were very impressed with what's going on here. Basically, what we started was just to go eat breakfast, and then we have our sons stand up and we say: 'This is my son Andy, and I'm most proud of him because . . .'"

At those gatherings, Bissmeyer would tell the sons and daughters assembled that nothing—of all the things they learned that day, that they saw or heard or experienced in any way—would match what they heard about themselves from the mouths of their fathers.

"I often thought if my father and I had gone to breakfasts like this when I was in high school, my life would've been changed," Fitzgerald figures.

Today, six years later, Fitzgerald advocates for All Pro Dad whenever requested and considers it a singular honor.

"Whatever All Pro Dad wants me to do, I'll be there," he says. "Wherever they want me to go, I'll go there. I'll speak. Because sometimes as Dads we don't do a very good job of letting our children know that we love them. When All Pro Dad came to Indianapolis and we told them about the program, they thought it was fantastic, which it is. So they went back and put organizational time and financial resources into promotion of the Dad's Day breakfast program, through their Web site, and made a DVD. What started in Indianapolis is a very good idea, but All Pro Dad really had the platform to reach out to so many more people."

Currently, more than seven hundred chapters of All Pro Dad exist internationally, beginning with a core base of more than two hundred in Florida alone, while Indiana claims seventy-five. There are even some in Iraq and one in India. Dads get together with kids before school and use a "Tony Dungy-powered" All Pro Dad's Day curriculum. All Pro Dad works with corporations like Chick-fil-A, hhgregg, Thrivent Financial for Lutherans, and others that help fuel the programs with their sponsorship. The idea is to inspire tens of thousands of dads to get up early in the morning with their kids and use this curriculum—a DVD series built on topics addressing perseverance, goal-setting, dealing with peer pressure, and faith issues.

"There are some tough issues, too, like sexual issues and other things that fathers are wrestling with," says All Pro Dad's Darrin Gray. "There are age-appropriate lessons. We've got curriculum that works from elementary all the way up to high school."

That is the All Pro Dad's Day platform. In addition, the outfit issues the world's most widely read fatherhood e-mail, called "The Play of the Day," a daily epistle containing hard-hitting information, advice, and inspiration to encourage fathers to be better dads. Currently, forty thousand families across America take "The Play of the Day" every day. The correspondence contains simple tips, arriving around lunchtime with the intent to catch dads—many of them sitting at their desks—not thinking about family. It provides a three-minute lesson on what a dad might do, ranging from tutorials on saving, spending, and sharing to stewardship of resources and how to schedule quality time.

"The footprint continues to grow as guys are adopting this football-themed platform of getting connected with their kids and staying that way," says Gray of the organization, which employs sixteen people out of the Tampa office and one full-time person each in Atlanta, Indianapolis, and Pittsburgh. "I was recently with the folks in the Vikings' office," Gray adds, "and my colleague is on the phone with the Chicago Bears as we speak, getting that event going with them. We're just so blessed to have Tony at the epicenter of this, really providing leadership and guidance to help us continue to move messages straight and true, and he's right in the middle of it."

Gray says that if you were to sit down and have a Coke with Dungy, he'd tell you he's seriously disturbed by what's happening to young African-American men, whose role models are often non-existent in their households, because in many cases the dads are absent. With rates of incarceration incredibly high, Dungy knows that, as an African American, he's in a unique position, as a father, community leader, and football coach to help inspire young people not to go down that path. As a youth, Dungy grew up in a prison town, Jackson, Michigan, home of the former State Prison of Southern Michigan—now the Southern Michigan Correctional Facility—once the largest walled prison in the world. Dungy's prison ministry has already been chronicled here, but the link between incarceration and father absenteeism in the home is unmistakable.

"Strengthening families is not easy," ascertains Gray, "but the things that we're doing are starting to take root. It's taken ten years—with Tony's help—to do that, but recently we've experienced an almost meteoric rise."

Recently Dungy was asked by President George W. Bush Jr. to get involved in programming that resulted in an initiative with White House representatives and the Governor of Indiana. Dungy came out and spoke on behalf of All Pro Dad. At the session, the Colts head coach also awarded a White House citation on behalf of the President's Council on Service and Civic Participation to Bissmeyer and Fitzgerald for their longstanding service to All Pro Dad.

"Tony's an amazing man who we just love and pray for," says Gray.

A city holds its breath

With the recent enrollment of the Dungy's son, Eric, in a Tampa high school, Dungy's wife of twenty-six years, Lauren, has moved back to that city permanently and become involved as a spokeswomen for Family First's motherhood program, iMom.com. Her relocation began a media swirl around Dungy's future with Indianapolis.

Following the Colts' deflating loss to San Diego in the 2007 divisional playoffs in the final game ever played at the RCA Dome, there was nonstop conjecture about Dungy's imminent departure from football, a logical extension given Lauren's move to Tampa and Dungy's long-ago promise to himself that he would spend no more than twenty-five years in the NFL. He had already eclipsed that, having given thirty years to the league as a player, assistant, and head coach through 2007.

An interminable week followed in mid-January for Colts fans waiting expectantly on the edge of their seats for word that would come on Monday, January 21, 2008—Martin Luther King Jr. Day— the day Dungy had designated to announce his decision regarding his future. Most pundits in the press fully expected him to retire, his world too large with other matters of importance, his rare skills as an inspirational motivator too much in demand to delay any longer his departure from the game for the broader universe of human aid.

"People in Indianapolis are sick to think that he may not be coaching," Fitzgerald said at the time. "I believe him when he says he doesn't see himself as a coach. It's just something he does, like the job we do. It's not necessarily who we are but something that we do to put bread on the table. For him, it's a platform to speak out to people that would normally not hear him."

For the moment, Gray could only keep on keepin' on. "We just continue to mobilize around Tony's needs and wishes and find ways for him to speak his truth and provide him with the forums to express himself relative to the importance of dads getting involved at events like the All Pro Dad Father and Kids Experience," says Gray. "It's no longer okay for dads to let moms do all the homework. It's no longer okay for moms to cook all the meals. We believe that there's an equally important role for men in this world, and there's a biblical basis to what we're doing."

At its annual banquet, All Pro Dad salutes excellence in fostering the father-child union with the Wilbur Dungy Award, in honor of Dungy's father, who passed away in 2004. Tony has spoken more than once of his disappointment in not being more of a hands-on father with his own children in the way that his dad had been for him. The two men's careers differed widely, with Wilbur always home for the day's duration after school let out. Tony's schedule as a pro football head coach by its very nature fails to lend itself to cheery family times at home during reasonable hours. A nine-to-five job it's not.

Gray has witnessed Dungy's deep respect for his father. "He admired his dad tremendously and speaks of him often," acknowledges Gray, "especially in the context I've seen him in, which is when we're reaching out to dads and to young people. He will say, 'I can't spend twenty-five percent as much time with my kids as my dad did with me.' In many cases, he's out working a whole lot of hours each week. In season, it's a real tough situation sometimes."

Fitzgerald, a past Wilbur Dungy Award cowinner, with friend

Bissmeyer, feels the exemplary qualities and stout beliefs engendered by Dungy are a perfect fit for the Colts coach's off-the-field endeavors.

"Tony being involved with All Pro Dad, he does it for the right reason," says Fitzgerald. "He's so sincere and everybody's so cynical nowadays, but when Tony Dungy says something, people just know that there's truth in what he's saying. It was so tragic when his son James died. Everybody died a little bit with him. But then he bounces back and his faith is so strong. It's so genuine, too. It doesn't change from one day to the other."

The Dungy Award is no small accolade to Fitzgerald. The man prizes the distinction honoring his service to fathers and sons.

"Bill and I were the second recipients to receive it," he says of the tribute. "Tony presented the awards to us, and you couldn't be any more honored than that. I can't imagine a greater honor, the way Tony speaks of his father. If there's anything you could ever be presented, that's about as high as it goes right there."

Fitzgerald has even gone so far as to place his champion in company with one of the world's unimpeachable icons of goodness.

"He's kind of like Mother Teresa," Fitzgerald offers. "You know how they said she would stop in an airport and talk to somebody who was just nobody she knew? She would think, 'Maybe God wants me to stop and talk to this person, and who am I to turn God's request down?' That's the way that Tony strikes me. He never hesitates to stop and talk to people. It doesn't matter if you're involved in football or not."

Mother Teresa would be proud: Those who know Dungy see an almost saint-like quality about him. "His players, when they talk about him, they're just in awe of him," says Fitzgerald. "People who are in a brutal industry like pro football, they're paid to smash people in the mouth—a Bob Sanders [Colts All-Pro safety] kind of person. But when they speak of Tony, their tone is gentle. They sound more like grandma speaking of him than they do football players. I think that's just a reflection of Tony and his demeanor. He's not, 'All right, we gotta get this thing done!' It's more like, 'We do what we do and we'll have do it a little bit better.'"

From his background and retreat experience, Fitzgerald has witnessed firsthand the "lousy" job that many men do in the role of dad, but he sees All Pro Dad as a vehicle to address such failings. He particularly laments the lack of attention given to daughters. When his youngest daughter left for college four years ago, it was the first time in thirty years that Fitzgerald didn't have a child at home to say, "How was your day at school today?"

"That hurt. We don't encourage them; we don't hold them anymore," Fitzgerald says of men's interactions with their daughters. "It's sad. One of the most precious gifts that God gives us is our children, and sometimes we're anxious to see them leave, or at least we act like we are, until they're gone."

To boost loving kindness in father-child relationships, Fitzgerald, at his talks, will have the children turn to their dads and say, "I love you." He then has the fathers respond, "I love you, too"—not "Me, too" or something less sincere—before giving their kid a sticker that says: "At Breakfast Today My Father Told Me that He Loves Me." The kids wear the message all day long at school, and when other kids ask about the sticker, it's an opening for them to say, "Come to breakfast next month." The kids also show it to their moms when they get home from school, before the child hides the sticker for later use as a bargaining chip. "The next time they get grounded for something, they can pull this out, and it's like a 'get out of jail free' card," explains Fitzgerald.

He also notes an interesting lesson gained from one of his own daughters about the seemingly harmless act of hugging. "The first time we went to a breakfast that was for dads and daughters, the speaker had us hold our daughters," recalls Fitzgerald. "I thought they were giving the speaker an ovation, but when I looked up it was the dads patting their daughters on the back. It sounded like applause. My daughter Lindsay leaned over to me and said, 'You know what that means in body language? It means 'I'm very uncomfortable doing this.' So I always warn the dads not to pat their daughters on the back when they're hugging them. Sometimes our kids have to tell us these things before we catch on."

In light of his own empty nest, Fitzgerald observes with a mixture of envy and awe the continuing growth of the Dungy family.

"The thing with Tony, he and Lauren keep adopting kids; they keep getting younger and younger," says Fitzgerald with a laugh. "Lauren's family adopted, and she taught Tony how to love kids like that, too. Who knows, twenty years from now they'll probably still have a three-year-old. That will keep people young."

The Dungys, in addition to their three—including Jamie—natural children, also have adopted three. Dungy quickly surrenders all credit to Lauren and her passionate heart. Tiara is now the oldest, followed by Eric, but the Dungys weren't through. Strong passions to adopt, as Fitzgerald mentioned, are almost a birthright for Lauren. Indeed, her parents set an incredible example, adopting throughout their lifetime. In their eighties, they currently raise an adopted child of middle-school age. The exposure to that wasn't lost on Lauren. Jordan, then Jade and Justin were pulled aboard the Good Ship Dungy. All have a wonderful grace about them.

"You know, they really do," says Dungy. "It is something that Lauren has carried the banner for and wanted to do, and she has that type of mind-set. She is just very special in that regard. The young kids are just so exciting to us. They have taught us so many things. Obviously we feel they are just a normal part of our family, but they have been kind of a special blessing."

The strength and constitution of Lauren has meant much to Dungy through all that the two have undergone. "She's been very, very special to our whole family," he says with the greatest admiration. "Just her mothering instincts in really taking care of our children, primarily during the season. That is something you can't even

fathom how important that is. She has been there as a support system for me and a person that loves me all the time and looks out for
me. I think that's what God gives you in a wife. I have been blessed
to have that for twenty-six years."

Dungy doesn't forget another blessing. It had been his kids'
extreme fortuity to have both sets of grandparents alive for a good
part of their young lives, before Dungy's parents passed. Says
Dungy, "I told my kids all the time, 'You guys are so fortunate; you
don't know how blessed you are!' At that time, to have both sets of
grandparents in their lives, who had both been married for more
than forty years, and have both set that kind of modeling for
them—it was great, not only for Lauren and I to see, but for our
kids to see. It's how it should be done."

"This is my son, and this is what I'm proud of"

For his superb efforts in helping others, Dungy is now getting to
glimpse the rewards of solid action in place and the good that can
come from that. An entire system of plans, strategies, and techniques
exist within All Pro Dad relative to scheduling time with kids. If the
procedures are adopted, according to Gray, practitioners will spend
both quality and quantity of time with their kids. One father benefiting from the All Pro Dad experience will never forget the impact a
simple breakfast with his son made on their lives together.

"My son, Nick, is sixteen and a junior," begins Steve Blaising,
forty-nine, half-owner of Brain Surgery Worldwide Inc., an emo-
tion-based marketing research company. "He's on the tennis team
at Cathedral High School here in Indianapolis. We were at a tennis
match last fall, and it just so happens my wife and I were in charge
of the treats that particular day. This gentleman came over towards
me at the end of the match and was having some snacks. It was Bill
Bissmeyer. He had lost his son, who also went to Cathedral. He
introduced himself to my son and told us we should come to a
breakfast tomorrow morning at six a.m. And I got to tell you, I

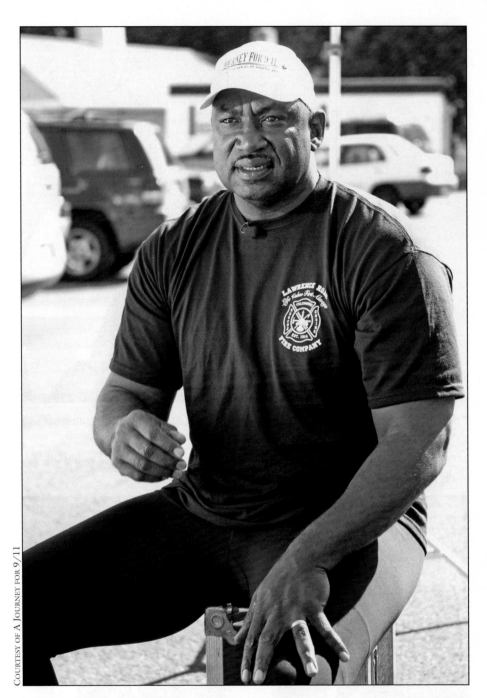

• Former New York Giants defensive end George Martin grabs a moment's rest during his Journey for 9/11 transcontinental walk to benefit seriously ill Ground Zero rescue and recovery workers, the "first responders" during the infamous terrorist attack of September 11, 2001.

- A Journey for 9/11 begins: George Martin (in blue ball cap at left above) is surrounded by well-wishers on New York's George Washington Bridge on September 16, 2007.

- Students (below) at Friendship Public Charter School in Washington, D.C., welcome Martin and the Journey team to the nation's capital.

- Despite 20-degree temperatures in Hicks Station, Arkansas, Martin (above) keeps his eye on the goal.

- Big George maintains a punishing pace in the rain (below) as traffic whizzes by, at times uncomfortably close.

- (Above) Residents of Sawyers Mill, Tennessee, celebrate the completion of the first 1,000 miles of Martin's Journey for 9/11.

- (Below) Martin kneels at the memorial outside the Murrah Federal Building in Oklahoma City.

• Bolstered by a strong Christian faith and an atypical coaching style that stresses personal responsibility and accountability, Tony Dungy encourages players to become leaders, both on and off the field.

• Dungy is a cofounder of All Pro Dad, a program that promotes strengthening families and making sure that dads step up to their most important mission: being a father. A frequent speaker at the organization's events, such as the All Pro Dad Father & Kids Experience hosted by the Indianapolis Colts pictured here, he is a gifted communicator in groups large and small.

- Warrick Dunn closed the 2007 season ranked twenty-third all time in NFL rushing yards, with 10,181 and counting, as he heads to Tampa Bay to begin his twelfth year in the league. But the three-time Pro Bowler places the well-being of others far ahead of gridiron milestones.

- (Above) Warrick Dunn assures emotionally overcome Habitat home recipient Jacquelyn "Grandma" Williams that the new dwelling is all hers.

- (Below) Dunn shows Tiffany Miles and children Jaiden and Tianna their home's fully equipped kitchen and stocked cupboards.

don't care who you say that to, that doesn't sound very appetizing. It's one thing to be awake at six and another thing to be somewhere. I thought, *You know, we should do that, we should do that.* We're driving home, and I said to Nick, 'Let's go tomorrow.' And of course Nick was, like, 'We'll see.' But I just kind of made a commitment: *Look, I'm going to get up at 4:45, and I'm going to get him up and we're going to go.* And so we did.

"The guy that played the lieutenant in *Miami Vice*, Edward James Olmos, happened to be the speaker that day. There's probably ten to fifteen tables full of dads and their sons, with a little buffet. You get some breakfast, sit down, and talk with everybody for a while. Then, this Bill Bissmeyer says, 'Now I want each of you dads to introduce yourself and then introduce your son and tell us what you are proud about regarding your son.' One by one, table by table, everybody stands up; you say who you are, you say, 'This is my son, and this is what I'm proud of.' At the end of that, he calls a couple kids out and he says, 'What did your dad say about you?' And they knew it word for word. Bill says, 'You know, dads, what you said you were most proud of about your sons today, they will remember word for word.' And he's not wrong.

"What happens when dads are introducing their sons is that the kids who are captain of the football team or the stud athletes in high school are brought down to a common denominator, if that make sense. When you're walking the halls of any high school, everybody puts on their own different face, and there's not a lot of authenticity about it. So [the dads breakfast] gets down to that core level, which is great. Bill puts my-father-told-me-he-loves-me stickers on all the boys. So, we're walking out the door of the cafeteria and Nick kisses me and says, 'I love you, Dad.' And you know, that's not an uncommon thing for he and I to say, but to do it in the middle of the hallway in school—that's pretty powerful.

"And I'm not the only one," Blaising continues. "That's a common thing if you watch what goes on. There's hugs, 'Have a good day, Son,' that kind of stuff. And we haven't missed since. It's a great way to start your day; it's fellowship. This is a cool thing. That was my experience. We have Nick's best friend and his dad now going. It's great."

In a world in which far too few precious moments can truly be counted, Blaising is thrilled for the chance to gain meaningful time with his son. "What struck me was that, without hesitation, this was an authentic moment between he and I; surroundings didn't matter," Blaising says. "When you're sixteen years old and you're around all your peers, boy, surroundings affect your behavior. Later that same day, I said, 'How did you like that?' Nick said, 'I really liked it. It was good. We should go back.'"

Blaising is obviously struck by the charismatic Bissmeyer and his innate sense of people and relationships. "He's doing it because he lost his son," says Blaising. "He'll look at your son and say, 'I see your wealth.' When you first hear that, you're kind of, *What is that all about?* But what he's saying is, the wealth is right there, it's your son! My son's no different than all those others. You get a hundred to a hundred-fifty people there—and these are high school freshmen, sophomores, juniors, seniors. Not long ago, because some of the colleges were still on break, some dads came with their college-age sons who used to attend. So you've got college kids there that used to come, you'll have grandfathers bringing their grandsons. We want the sons there. If there isn't a dad in the family, we've had moms bring their sons.

"But you get something out of it. If you're not fed, you don't come back. So there's an authenticity there, it's a bonding thing, and it starts your day off great. If a young person can have other adults that they can be friends with, that's a big deal. One of the things that happens here is that these kids also get to meet other dads. It's a stake in the ground."

The wide scope of father-son interaction that All Pro Dad generates even produced an odd surprise for Dungy, who recalls an

unlikely but welcome connection with his early mentor Leroy Rocquemore via correspondence sent to the organization.

"His son wrote a letter to the president of Family First," Dungy
says of Rocquemore, who long ago helped repair a fractured relationship between Dungy and his high school football coach. "He
said, 'Hey, I knew Tony Dungy when he was little. I remember one
of my last memories was of him stopping by my house. He had
some conversation with my dad; I don't know what it was all about.
I just remember him coming over and saying hi when he was a senior in high school.' It just really is an unbelievable coincidence for
Mark Merrill to get this letter forty years later."

Gray remembers an instance in which the even-keeled Dungy
exhibited a shining example of patience at a tough time, placing his
admirable principles on display while fulfilling an appearance obliga-
tion for All Pro Dad.

"Back in Week Nine [2007], the Colts were getting ready to
play a big game against the New England Patriots," recalls Gray.
"Everybody was calling it Super Bowl XLI $\frac{1}{2}$. The day before, on
Saturday, we had nearly two thousand fathers and young people
come to the practice facility, and Tony was there from the beginning
until the end, speaking, signing autographs, doing photo ops,
engaging with the folks in so many interesting ways. He was there
with that calm, quiet presence we so value. The next day we all went
to the game and enjoyed it, but we came up on the short end [Pats
24, Indy 20]. Tony didn't get upset, he was just calm and there.

"The very next day, we had that event in downtown Indianapolis with the White House and the governor of Indiana. Tony met
me that next morning and we held a press conference with the
bright lights and all, and Tony's just the same—with that quiet,
calm passion for fatherhood that he displayed on the Saturday
before the game, with the game on Game Day, the loss, and then
showing up for the White House initiative on Monday. It's an
example of Tony's ongoing commitment. He didn't have to do

that. He can certainly find other things to do with his time. It would all be good, right, and true. But he can help people and he wants to, and he does."

No matter who is doing the talking, it seems there is unanimity among players and NFL contemporaries about the depth of Dungy's humanity. Colts players, of course, are in the direct line of fire—or direct line of peace, actually. Gray recalls the comments of Hunter Smith, a spokesman for All Pro Dad entering his tenth year as Indy's punter, whose respect and admiration for Dungy is typical of the team's devotion to its coach.

"I've have had long conversations with Hunter about Tony and the influence that Tony has had on young players and on him specifically," says Gray. "Hunter's like, 'We'll climb a mountain for this guy, we'll do anything for this guy, we know that he would never lead us astray.' And that's the difference: he's a player, Tony's a player's coach, and these guys love him. His influence is so wide. I had a long conversation with Mike Tomlin in Pittsburgh about Tony. They love this guy. I've never seen this sort of allegiance to an NFL character in quite this same way. Other coaches, their players maybe admire them or revere them, but there's this interesting balance in Tony that is all of those things. Well beyond reverence and respect, these guys will do anything for Tony."

Center Jeff Saturday feels that exposure to Dungy and his impeccable ways can be contagious. He and all the Colts players have had regular opportunities to see Dungy the family man up close and personal, even in the workplace. Or perhaps, *especially* in the workplace.

"People realize how much he cares about others, and that's addictive," says the three-time All-Pro of his boss. "When people see other people give up their lives to help people, I think that catches on. He does a good job of allowing people to see him in the act; that then encourages people to go step out and do it themselves, and that's always an encouragement. I know for myself, being a parent of three children, I watch what he does. I watch how he has to live his life. When he brings his kids to the complex, and they're playing PlayStation in his office, and all the different things he'll do when he has them there, and then they'll go out on the field. I know I have a great deal of respect for that, because those times you will never have back with your children. He is willing to sacrifice being 100 percent focused on football for that ten hours, or whatever it may be, to share that time with his family.

"I know how often teaching moments come up for kids when you're in situations like that—when you can teach them how to shake another man's hand and look him in the eye, and teach them how to be respectful when other people are talking to people—all the little things you teach your kids as they move along in their lives. He has the opportunity and he does it; he takes advantage of it, even in the locker room. I have a lot of respect for that, and I think it is a great way to show kids, *Hey listen, look how hard these guys work, and look what they have to do. Here are the men you should respect, and here is why.* Just those small teaching moments, he takes advantage of that, and it's a great way to follow parenting steps from what he does."

With his commitment to all things dad and son, you might wonder how Dungy's personal code comes across to the Colts, especially the younger players who may not have started families of their own.

"Men who are parents on the team, who have kids and have wives, I think they can see a whole lot more about Tony right now," observes Saturday. "Men who are going to have kids later on—once they have their family and have the responsibilities—they will appreciate Tony even more than they do now, as much they already appreciate him. They will realize how much he is managing at one time, and how difficult it is to balance family and football and your faith and all the different responsibilities that you have, and how good he is at doing it. And how *quiet* he is in doing it."

The latter remark is poignant. It is not just relative to Dungy but also the other off-the-field heroes recounted in this book. Not one of them openly seeks publicity for his good works. Though all realize that a certain amount of attention comes with the turf, the thought of actively lobbying for publicity is anathema to them. And the workload, it's just stunning. For Dungy, there's never any shortage of projects to involve his time for benevolent causes.

"It never ceases to amaze me, the number of programs and connections that Tony can make," says Gray, who mentions that Dungy, in the summer of 2008, will follow up *Quiet Strength*, the No. 1 *New York Times* best-seller, with a new book for children, *You Can Do It*. "He just continues to find ways to touch people."

In the kind of out-of-place paradox that finds its way into many of life's incongruous situations, Dungy admits to harboring doubts, almost pangs of unworthiness, about his efficacy as a spokesman for All Pro Dad after his son took his own life.

"How ironic," Dungy mentions in *Quiet Strength*. "Here I am, a spokesman for the All Pro Dad program, helping others be better parents, and my child took his own life. I figured this would wipe out any credibility I might have had."

Dungy underestimated himself, and certainly others, including parents "who had been there." The outpouring of sympathy and condolences in the aftermath of Jamie's death from those who had experienced similar pain and loss was humbling to the man.

"I had always said that football was my job but that it was not the most important thing in my life," Dungy reiterated. "Jamie's death had reinforced that. Now I would learn if my faith and my ideals would hold up when put to the test."

Chapter Ten

BLACK MARKS
ON THE NFL

When the NFL was in its so-called Golden Era—the 1950s—the raciest stories about pro football heroes reaching the public's ears usually drifted out of summer training camps. Tales grew into legend and then myth on the sizable drinking capacities of some players, and the script for reaching that sought-after state of inebriation usually ran the same: Sneak out of the dorm after curfew and head for the suds at the nearest tavern. Intermixed with robust beer drinking was the customary clubhouse pastime of prank playing. Stars such as Bobby Layne, Paul Hornung, Max McGee, Fred Biletnikoff, Ken Stabler, and countless others gained stout reputations as party animals to go hand in hand with their glittering statistics and championship rings.

But it seems the list of off-the-field antics, bad judgment, questionable conduct, and out-and-out criminal activity by league players has burgeoned and darkened in recent years. In April 2007, NFL Commissioner Roger Goodell suspended Cincinnati Bengals wide receiver Chris Henry for the first eight games of the 2007 season for violating the league's personal-conduct policies. The series of indiscretions leading up to that decision included:

- December 15, 2005—Henry is pulled over in northern Kentucky for speeding. Marijuana is found in his shoes. He is also driving without a valid driver's license, and without auto insurance.
- January 30, 2006—Henry is arrested in Orlando, Florida, on multiple gun charges, including concealment and aggravated assault with a firearm. He pleads guilty and avoids jail time.
- May 4, 2006—Cincinnati media report Henry is being investigated by police in connection with a sex crime, which allegedly occurred in a hotel room in Covington, Kentucky, early on April 30, 2006. No charges are filed, and on May 24, Covington police state that there is no proof anything happened and that the alleged victim might face charges for filing a false police report.
- June 3, 2006—Henry is pulled over on Interstate 275 at 1:18 a.m. by Ohio state police. He voluntarily submits to a breathalyzer test and registers a .092 blood-alcohol level, .012 above the state's legal limit. Charges are later dismissed, the breathalyzer proving to be faulty.
- October 6, 2006—Henry is suspended by the NFL for two games for violating the league's personal-conduct and substance-abuse policies. NFL policies forbid Henry from taking part in practices. He misses the Bengals' October 15 game at Tampa Bay and the October 22 game against Carolina.
- January 25, 2007—Henry pleads guilty to charges of providing alcohol to minors, the incident occurring at a hotel in the spring of 2006. He is sentenced to ninety days in jail, with all but two of those days being suspended.

Although Henry's suspension came with a stern warning that future misconduct might result in the end of his career with the NFL, he soon was embroiled in more controversy. On May 18, 2007, Henry allegedly failed a court-mandated drug test, when a field test resulted in a false positive for taking an opiate, according to the *Cincinnati Enquirer*. The failed drug test would have been his third violation of the NFL's substance-abuse policy, which, per league rules, would mean a mandatory one-year suspension. In addition to having his suspension increased to twenty-four games, he would be required to serve an eighty-eight-day jail sentence. On May 23, 2007, the State of Kentucky reported that Henry in fact did *not* fail a drug test, and that earlier reports to the contrary were erroneous.

A few weeks later, on June 12, Henry and teammate Reggie McNeal are accused of assaulting a sixteen-year-old boy. The claims are later reported to be unfounded, and Henry and McNeal are exonerated. On November 6, Henry was again in the news for allegedly assaulting a valet parking attendant at a popular entertainment attraction in Newport, Kentucky. Henry was not charged in the incident. Then, on April 1, 2008, he was arrested on misdemeanor assault and criminal damaging charges stemming from an altercation in Cincinnati. Bengals President Mike Brown had had enough, and the following day the team parted ways with Henry.

Yet Henry's list of dubious accomplishments pales in comparison to the less-than-exemplary actions of former Tennessee Titans cornerback Adam "Pacman" Jones, a Pro Bowl player in 2006, whose involvement in violent crime harkens back to the gray days of Ray Lewis and his thuggish entourage of the early 2000s. Jones, arrested six times and interviewed a dozen times by police, has not been convicted of any crimes. However, his involvement in a much-publicized shooting incident in February 2007 that left a Las Vegas club employee paralyzed led Commissioner Goodell to tell Jones to take a seat for the entire 2007 season. The suspension required that Jones have "no further adverse involvement with law enforcement."

The Titans, à la Cincinnati's Brown, waved the white flag and dealt the troubled corner to Dallas in the 2007-08 off-season. Now it's the Cowboys who will be Jonesing. Jones-to-Jones. Cowboys owner Jerry, acting every bit the modern-day equivalent of an earlier Al Davis, is now stocking up on NFL miscreants, having signed Tank Johnson last year, after a succession of ill-advised incidents in Chicago compelled the Bears to dump the problematic defensive tackle.

But Henry's and Jones's grimy laundry was snow white compared to the dark and sinister unfolding that surfaced around former Atlanta Falcons quarterback Michael Vick's celebrated involvement in a dog-fighting ring in early summer 2007. Suddenly, the image-conscious NFL was having a serious image problem. The brooding cruelty of the Vick incident and the public's sharp response generated a new high in negative publicity for the NFL. A somewhat hopeful tidbit appearing on Dan Patrick's page in the March 24, 2008, issue of *Sports Illustrated* announced that personal misconduct incidents were down 20 percent in the past year, according to a league report. That upbeat intelligence was then glibly followed by a parenthetical remark stating that was the case "largely because so many players are already in jail."

Alongside the abovementioned nefarious antics, Dungy is a dolphin in a pool of sharks. As you might imagine, the Colts' head coach has a more accepting view of sinners and lawbreakers, an understanding due in part to his awareness of dead-end origins for many NFL players and the less-than-optimal family and support circumstances prevailing in Poor America that initially condition the young.

"Most of our players are really tremendous young men," says Dungy. "The percentage is so high, because you don't make it in the NFL without having some strength of character. But what our players have to understand is that the biggest thing we've got going for us is the confidence of the public, and that confidence comes from the way we are viewed. So, any incident that chips away at that confidence is very, very difficult on everyone. We've got a responsibility not only to be role models for young men, which is so important, but also to continue to grow our game, and it is not going to grow if the public thinks *Hey, they've got a bunch of guys who are out of control, so that's not going to be good.* We have to understand that. We've got to educate our players and do a good job that way. It has got to come from the older players, it's got to come from the coaches; it's got to come from the league and everyone.

"I think Commissioner Goodell is on the right track. Bad decisions can happen with players, everyone. But your judgment at twenty-one is not going to be the same as your judgment at thirty-one, forty-one or fifty-one. Just like with your family and your children, you have to have rules and parameters and guidelines and discipline should they go outside those things. Then you have to have the nurturing side to help people grow and help your kids grow, and you can't have one without the other. You can't just be all nurturing and say, 'oh, that's okay, everybody makes mistakes,' but you can't have just the other side either, where it is all discipline, punishment, and parameters, and if you go outside the box you're finished. It's got to be a balance. That's what we have got to have."

Looking down the line, Dungy sees a hopeful future tended to by conscientious attitudes. "I try to get across to our players that you are going to have a lot of people that look at you and admire you for how you play," he says, "but in the long run it is important, especially for our young boys, to be able to look up at you and admire you for what else you do, how you do things, how you live. That's what we've got to set the course for, for the next generation. Fortunately we've got a lot of guys who believe that."

Tony Dungy talks with Indianapolis telejournalist Lyndsay Clutter of WTHR 13 during the All Pro Dad Father & Kids Experience.

Walking the walk

The Colts' coach isn't one to separate his personal beliefs from the role he inhabits on the field. His emotional consistency is a steadying influence on the players, and he's not shy to pull out Bible chapter and verse to illustrate a point or to inspire his squad with one of scripture's many episodic accounts. A tale that all have grown up with from birth served as the perfect motivator during the team's 2006 championship run, when Indianapolis had to face its biggest foe, New England, to advance to the Super Bowl.

Dungy concedes that, while winning Super Bowl XLI was terrific, downing the Chicago Bears didn't match the emotional enormity of that season's American Football Conference Championship Game. That contest was a conquest, a long-overdue mission accomplished. The Patriots, the eternal thorn in the Colts' postseason side, had pushed Indianapolis out of the playoffs twice in two previous years. To inspire his team for the upcoming battle, Dungy used a story he'd heard his mother tell many times in his youth—the epic account of David and Goliath, the proverbial tale of the underdog slaying the giant.

"That's what came across my mind, that we had someone out there who seemed a little bigger than life," says Dungy of New England, finally tamed by Indianapolis, 38–34. "They really aren't, but that is the perception. So David and Goliath was easy to come up with."

Maintaining motivation isn't a task unique to Dungy. All NFL coaches face the trial. At the cornerstone of Dungy's longtime philosophy, now thoroughly ingrained in his players, are two carefully honed maxims that have become the coach's and the Colts' mission statement: "Do what we do," and "Stay the course." The former, a challenge not to abandon the principles that work for the team, too often is ignored in the nothing-matters-but-winning world of the NFL. Clubs that get close but fall short of the big prize begin to jettison elements of their game that may well be their foundation pins. "Do what do we" simply urges players to concentrate on the basics and perform them better.

Like a seaman in rough storms, Dungy puts on his captain's hat when exhorting his charges to "stay the course"—a dig-deep-down reminder that he who is strong in the fourth quarter, who sucks it up with both physical and mental toughness over the long haul, will emerge the victor. The dual philosophy, not surprisingly, is rooted in the tenets of the Book of Noll.

"It really came through Coach Noll and [Steelers assistant coach] Benny Green, two guys who I worked for the longest," says Dungy of his early mentors. "That is what they both believed in. Coach Noll used to say it all the time: You have something you believe in, you got to stick to it. You can't leave it, because when you do, everyone is going to see through it. He used to always think that if we got ourselves ready to play at our level, it didn't really matter who we were playing. The games we were going to lose weren't going to be because of the opponent, they were going to be because we didn't function as well as we could. That kind of became my mantra over the years—that if we could really focus in, dial in on what we do, not change, not be up and down, but be very consistent, then we were going to be fine."

From a player's perspective, Dungy's philosophy has to be comforting. Athletes blowing an assignment aren't going to get their heads flattened or lose their starting position because of temporary incompetence or error. On the contrary, that unpressured reassurance tends to bond the team.

"I think it does, and I felt that from Coach Noll," says Dungy. "I didn't know it when I played for him, but when I came on his staff I understood his thought process. He said, 'You know, when everybody is getting attacked, that's when you lose.' You can do your best teaching when you win. When everybody is patting players on the back and telling them how good they are, that's when you need to get your point across: 'Here is what we need to do better.' When you are not winning, that's when you need encouragement to stay the course. Everybody on the outside is telling the player, 'You need to change this, you need to do that differently, this isn't working.' They just need the encouragement. No, we don't need to change, we just need to sharpen what we always do."

The best principles, however, will carry a team only so far. Losses, the bane of the sporting fraternity, eventually alter the landscape of any NFL team, its coach, and its players.

"One of the most difficult challenges in football is for the loser of a big game to come back the following year and reach the same height," Dungy has said. "It's difficult for winners as well. The pressure to repeat is intense."

Dungy and the Colts found that out in the ultimately disappointing 2007 season. After falling to arch-nemesis New England in the middle of the Patriots' perfect regular-season run and losing highly valued stars Marvin Harrison and Dwight Freeney to injury,

Indianapolis still entered the postseason as the prohibitive favorite to offer challenge to New England's unmistakable supremacy. But in a mildly surprising upset in the AFC Divisional Playoffs, the not-at-full-strength Colts bowed to a charged-up Chargers team that had beaten Indy handily during the regular season.

The Colts at least know that they will have the services of their indomitable leader for at least the 2008 season and possibly longer, after the welcomed announcement by Dungy at the Martin Luther King Jr. Day press conference that had many fans holding their breath. In this age of here-today-gone-tomorrow coaches, Dungy is a rarity: a coach who failed to defend his Super Bowl title whom *everyone* wanted back—players, assistant coaches, fans, and administrators. The state of Dungy's off-the-field interests, specifically his community and philanthropic work, is such that many people close to him felt he was finally going to put his twenty-seven-year NFL coaching career behind him to concentrate full time on his worthy charitable endeavors, including All Pro Dad.

Though he made no mention of acute inner turmoil surrounding his decision to stay with the Colts for 2008, Dungy confesses he experiences frustration at not hearing directly from God during moments of strife. "Over and over in life I've looked for that moment captured by Cecil B. DeMille in *The Ten Commandments*, when I could hear that same voice of God so clearly heard by Moses at the edge of the Red Sea: 'Go this way, and I'll part the waters for you.' But there has been no such moment. I have yet to hear God's audible voice."

Dungy's feeling on that subject sparks a personal recollection. While writing an earlier book on the life of Reggie White, I ran across many chronicled instances where the late Hall of Fame defensive end and ordained minister claimed to have "talked with God," at times participating in what appeared to be almost a running dialogue with the Almighty. No such banter with God has manifested itself yet in Dungy's life. In one instance—while praying for guidance on a career-choice matter—Dungy sought higher interaction. Typically, he was served with silence.

"As usual, there was no clear voice from God—not even a muffled murmur," he recounted in his book. Instead, he is of the belief that God's Word courses through the wiring that we are given from birth. "The people we talked to kept coming back to the same thing: follow your passion."

Chillin' with the fourteen days

Tony Dungy's life, while inspirational on all fronts, might lead some to wonder if he ever gets a rest from the serious business of coaching a pro football team and helping others in myriad ways. There is a lighter side to Dungy, and at times, acquaintances get a glimpse of his droll wit. Jeff Saturday, the Colts' offensive-line mainstay and a selectee to noted sports journalist/historian Paul Zimmerman's 2007 All-Pro Team, recounts a humorous/curious episode regarding his coach and mentor.

"If you know football, this would be humorous," starts Saturday. "You know Tony, you know how quiet he is and how genuinely nice a man he is. He is always like that, always a gentleman when you are around. Well, I had to go into his office one day on behalf of the players to try and change some stuff in our off-season conditioning program. He will always hear you out, but it doesn't necessarily mean he is going to change. If he feels like what he is doing is right, he will make you *feel* like he is going to change it. He'll be looking at you and you're talking to him, and you're like, 'Do you understand what I'm saying?' and he'll say, 'Oh, I totally understand what you mean, I understand how you are feeling about that.'

"The point of my going in was to attempt to shrink down what we call our fourteen OTA days—on-the-field activities—to get them to be fewer," Saturday continues. "The veteran guys wanted the OTA days shrunk down, because it goes over a lot of things we have already done. It would be more beneficial for the rookies to get that. So, I was talking to him and I kept saying, 'You know, if you could get the veterans fewer days and just let the rookies continue to do everything, we will set a good standard by coming in the first few days and then maybe sporadically through a couple days of practice here and there.'

"But he kept going back to the fourteen days. He would be like, 'I really understand, I like your idea, it is a great idea, but how are we going to get our fourteen days in?' We just started laughing, and finally I was like, 'I don't think we can get the fourteen days in totally for the guys.' But he kept going back to it. It got humorous because I kept trying to say something and he would hear it, but at the end it was still 'I like it, but how can we get the fourteen days?'

"He always hears you out. He always listens, he is a great listener. He always makes you feel like you are being heard and that it counts, that it matters. So he's looking at me, very intent: 'Yeah, absolutely, I love the idea, I think it's great!' But he just kept chillin' with the fourteen days. I just laughed and he looked at me, and I was like, 'All right, the fourteen days is our hang-up.'"

Saturday laughs when it is suggested that a man like Tony Dungy couldn't have hung around Chuck Noll as much as he did and not have picked up some steel-rod fortitude along the way.

"I think he still has Chuck Noll's schedules and we still go by them," Saturday chuckles. "I think it's really the way we roll."

Chapter Eleven

"Hug 'Em Every Chance You Get"

W ednesday, December 28, 2005. It is a sunlit day in Lutz, Florida, just north of Tampa, and more than two thousand mourners are convening at Idlewild Baptist Church to pay their last respects to eighteen-year-old Jamie Dungy. During the emotional two-hour funeral service—the Dungys prefer to call it Jamie's homecoming—his father will talk for twenty minutes. NFL stars past and present, league officials, including Commissioner Paul Tagliabue, and the entire Colts team are among those in attendance.

In his remarks, Dungy addresses his Colts players, the entire team assembled in the front rows directly across from the Dungy family. He hails them as "great role models," and advocates that they reach out even more.

"I want to urge you to continue being who you are because our young boys in this country, they need to hear from you," he says to them. "If anything, be bolder in who you are, because our boys are getting a lot of the wrong messages about what it means to be a man in this world. About how you should act, and how you should dress, and how you should talk, and how you should treat people. They don't always get the right message, but you guys have the right messages."

In talking about Jamie, Dungy says he is saddened that he didn't get to hug him the last time he saw him. It was at the airport, at Thanksgiving, and it was only going to be a short time before they saw each other again at Christmas. But there was no next time. The missed hug haunts Dungy, and he tells people that.

"I never got to hug him again," he laments to the mourners. "Parents, hug your kids every chance you get. That's one thing I'll always think about and always remind people to do: Hug 'em every chance you get. Tell them you love them every chance you get. You don't know when it's going to be the last time."

Abe Brown, who has seen Dungy cast a spell over prison inmates with his genuineness and sincerity, observed an awesome display of inner strength and courage as the Dungys literally stood tall through their painful ordeal.

"I stood with him the night that he was kind enough to have the wake in the ghetto, where our church is," recalls Brown. "They used the wake at the funeral home so they could shake hands with just the common people—the drug addicts, the losers, and the average people in the midst of the black community. An ordinary person would have had the wake in another place more convenient and out of the path of the people of that description. He had his wake right in the midst of the ghetto community. Not only did he have the wake there, but he stood for *four* hours. His wife stood in heels, and he stood and embraced and hugged everybody that came in.

"They started about six p.m. and had it scheduled to finish at eight o'clock. Well, I want you to know that when eight o'clock comes, there were people still in line. They tried to get him to close the doors, and he wouldn't do it. He was not going to stop until everybody had had the opportunity to come through and be embraced. He stood there; I stood there with him. He stood there *four hours.* His wife stood in *heels!* He didn't stop to even go to the bathroom. It was unrealistic. You just don't find people like that."

Following the service the next day, before leaving for the cemetery, Dungy exhibits more impressive restraint and self-control, making a brief statement outside the church and, on behalf of his wife, Lauren, and family, thanking friends and fans for their support. Jeff Saturday remembers another group present whom Dungy thanked for their consideration, a contingent not generally regarded for their courtesy or caring concern.

"He goes outside to the media and addresses them. He tells the media, 'Thank you for being here,'" says Saturday incredulously. "Those kinds of things, they just blow you away. You sit back and go, 'I can't even imagine being that mature in my faith.' It's just mind-boggling."

After the homecoming and following the painful three-point loss to Pittsburgh in the 2005 AFC Divisional Playoffs, Saturday recollects how the entire experience provided him with yet more glimpses into the wonder of his coach.

"After Jamie had just passed away and we had lost to the Steelers, we obviously went through a difficult time as a team but nothing even close in comparison to what he had lost," recalls Saturday. "I really felt like he had experienced a double whammy. I mean, how awful losing your son must be. But then you come back and you're favored and you're at home for the divisional playoff, with all those advantages, and everybody's talking about 'Oh, this is their time, and for sure they're going to be a shoo-in.' But we just get beat by Pittsburgh, and there's the difficulty of all that for him [Dungy] career-wise. I went into him and just really shared my heart about the way that he conducted himself after he lost Jamie and the way that he handled himself.

"I remember I called him the day that Jamie passed," Saturday continues. "Peyton [Manning] called me early in the morning on my way to work, and I called Tony after that. They were going down to Tampa to make sure it was Jamie and to meet with the police and all those kinds of things. I called to leave him a message; it was just to tell him that I was praying for him and that I loved him and Lauren and his family, and that if there was anything we could do for them, we would do it. But, he answered the phone! I remember just being shocked. I can't imagine answering the phone under those circumstances, and there's no way I would have. The phone would have been the farthest thing from my mind. But now he answers the phone, so I just shared my heart with him at that moment.

"After the funeral, after the season, I remember going back and again sharing with him as a fellow believer. The way he turned Jamie's funeral into a celebration for Christ and how he used it as a witness and a testimony, his behavior, the way he conducted himself as a Christian—all of it motivated me to be a better father, a better man, and most importantly, a better Christian. The maturity that I saw in his walk with Christ made it that much more real to me. If there is any compliment I could ever give a man, it is that his walk with Christ makes it real, it makes it a tangible thing that you can see and grab and get ahold of. In the most difficult time of his life, he never wavered and he never was shaken. I told him that face to face in his office. We shook hands and hugged, and he said, 'I really thank you for saying that.' It was probably one of the greater moments of my life, just to be able to share with another man how he has impacted me. And we have a professional relationship; this is still a boss-employee relationship. To be able to tell somebody that, and to mean it, it couldn't have been more heartfelt. How impressed I was in the way he handled it all.

"It charged me to be better in my life and to do the things he spoke of during the funeral, of always loving your kids and always telling them you love them before they leave—all the little things that he said. You know, I've got three young children. When he shared his stories [at the funeral] about Jamie growing up, that is where I am in my life. I've looked at it and just thanked God that somebody could say that and be that honest in their most difficult time, so that I could benefit and could help my family benefit. One of the greater things I have been through and been a part of was to watch Christ be revealed in Tony's life and in who he is and his family."

Incredibly, just a week to the day after young Jamie died, Dungy was back at work. "As painful as it was," Dungy says, "getting back into our routine was important. Work would help take my mind off my own pain, but I wanted to make sure that Lauren and the kids were as emotionally stable as possible under the circumstances."

More than two years removed from the tragedy, Dungy is even-minded and practical in his carriage of the event. "What we have always tried to do is just look forward and to grow from it," he says.

For obvious reasons, the subject is not a topic that the Dungys wish to dwell upon. Yet some of the messages inherent in it cannot be ignored. "I think it has made us a little more observant, being careful and enjoying everyday with our other children," Dungy says. "It has given us a platform to talk with other people. There have been some positives that we've seen out of it, some relationships that I have formed with parents that have been in the same situation, who have lost kids. Why it happened exactly, we'll never know. But I do know it has made me not take any day, any thing for granted."

Brown, Dungy's Tampa compatriot, succinctly sums up the magnitude of his good friend.

"He is truly a man of God and he is a blessing, not only to the football world, but to those who are less fortunate."

The blogger d9a2v4, who long ago faced Dungy on the football field as an eighth-grader, senses that special acclaim and a rare status lie ahead for the Indianapolis head coach. "I am not ashamed to say that I cried when I heard the news about his son James," the man notes. "Tony Dungy was put on earth to become much, much more than a professional football coach. It is ironic that I first met Tony Dungy in 1968, the year Martin Luther King was assassinated and Muhammad Ali was in the midst of getting back into boxing after having his title stripped for embracing his conscience and being an objector to the Vietnam War draft. My prediction is that Tony Dungy will obtain a social status equal to both King and Ali before he is through."

⚬⚬⚬ ⚬⚬⚬ ⚬⚬⚬

Asked how he hopes people will best remember him, Dungy says, "You know, I was asked that question recently and I had to think about it. I was on a speaking engagement, and I said, 'I hope they would remember me not as a person who developed good football players but as a person who made an impact in the community, made the places that I worked better places to live, and really helped develop young men that I worked with to be better parts of the community that we lived in.'"

PART THREE

WARRICK DUNN

Noble Enabler

Chapter Twelve

A MOTHER'S DREAM

It may seem a little simplistic, yet fittingly appropriate, to use a favorite children's analogy to help describe a facet of Warrick Dunn. Remember when you were little and a loved one would say, "Do you know how much you are loved?" You might have shaken your head or shrugged your shoulders or even said in return, "How much?" The person would then spread their arms out as wide as they could and say, "This much!" Well, if you were asked to measure the size of Dunn's heart, you might well be stretching the ligaments in your shoulders to illustrate the enormity of the man's love and generosity.

For the past eleven years, the three-time Pro Bowler, through his Warrick Dunn Foundation, has been an instrument of unconditional altruism. His "Homes for the Holidays" program provides first-time pre-qualified home buyers, who are associated with an approved nonprofit organization, with down-payment assistance on their new home. Dunn's sponsors also donate a striking interior package that includes such start-up offerings as brand-new furniture for every room; washer, dryer and refrigerator; a fully stocked kitchen with an array of appliances and dishware; linens; lawn and garden equipment; home-decor items; and even cleaning supplies.

One only has to see the reaction of people on the receiving end of Dunn's generosity to realize the huge impact the program creates. Yet, as Dunn stresses, this is no handout. In fact, his assistance is a play on an ancient proverb: Dunn helps those who help themselves, since all prospective buyers have invested hundreds of sweat-equity hours into the building of their own home. And if you're thinking Dunn probably just lends his name to this deserving cause, guess again.

"We receive nominations, and I read each story to see which nominees have been working hard to achieve home ownership," he says.

Dunn relishes his task, feeling praise for such work is an unnecessary complication. "I think that everyone should give back, and they should do it without the need for recognition and praise," he says, emphasizing that he wasn't placed on earth just to play football.

Not that what he does on the football field isn't special. The mercurial running back is entering his twelfth NFL season, the six previous ones with the Atlanta Falcons, before being released during the 2007–08 off-season, then serendipitously resigning with the club he had originally starred for in the late 1990s, Tampa Bay. Over that span he has solidly established himself as one of the league's premier all-purpose backs. Few players in the NFL can boast a national collegiate championship ring, a Super Bowl ring, and three selections to the Pro Bowl. More curiously, Dunn, a diminutive five-foot-eight, 178-pounder with the skittery moves of a waterbug, is that rare commodity for a ball carrier in the rugged NFL: a durable back. It has allowed him to accumulate some impressive career statistics, including a major milestone that he was closing in on as the 2007 Thanksgiving holidays approached.

But first, how is it that this man should come to this place in his life, giving away checks like John Beresford Tipton in the old TV series *The Millionaire*? As with so many people who embark on a path of caring and aid, a cataclysmic event altered his life at a young and tender age.

On Thursday, January 7, 1993, Corporal Betty Dunn Smothers, a fourteen-year officer with the Baton Rouge City Police Department, was shot and killed in an ambush while moonlighting as a security guard. She was in uniform and driving a marked patrol car, escorting a store manager to a bank to make a night deposit. As they sat in the car, three suspects approached and opened fire, fatally wounding Dunn's mother and injuring the manager. All three suspects were arrested after the incident.

In addition to the two daughters and four sons left behind, a lifelong dream of Smothers was also extinguished: She had always hoped to one day own her own home to provide a secure haven for her children. It is that unfulfilled wish of his mom's that fueled Dunn to eventually begin the Homes for the Holidays program. But it wasn't as simple as that.

Warrick Dunn immediately went from being cared for to becoming male head of household. Along with his grandmother, Willie Wheeler, he was now "parent" and provider—at just eighteen years of age. As an All-America honorable-mention selection by *USA Today* his senior year at Catholic High School in Baton Rouge, playing cornerback, quarterback, and running back, Dunn drew attention from several major universities. But how would he make it through college—plus support his three brothers and two sisters— on an NCAA athletic scholarship that doesn't permit its recipients to earn more than a pittance from traditional school-related employment or outside part-time jobs?

"The local community of Baton Rouge came together to establish a trust fund for our family," says Dunn of one of the few bright spots in the nightmarish aftermath of his mother's murder. "It was not easy," he recalls of the turbulent period, "and it made me grow up fast."

Bobby Bowden, the legendary head coach at Florida State, reassured Dunn that, despite the youth's thoughts of quitting college altogether, Dunn's place was at FSU. It turned out to be the right call, as Dunn rocketed into the limelight as the featured back in the Seminoles' offense, becoming a three-time first team All-ACC selection, as well as the first player in Seminoles history to record three 1,000-yard rushing seasons.

Following his outstanding success in Tallahassee, Dunn caught the eye of new Tampa Bay Buccaneers head coach Tony Dungy, who was looking to draft a running back that "could hit home runs." Tampa Bay's No. 1 pick in the 1995 draft, outside linebacker Derrick Brooks—an FSU alum—had touted Dunn to Dungy whenever the chance arose. The Bucs' mentor recalls the first time he met Dunn, at the NFL Scouting Combine in Indianapolis in late February 1997.

"I came away from our initial meeting highly impressed," recalls Dungy in his tome *Quiet Strength*. "I was around him for only about twenty minutes, but I left with the feeling that this guy could be something really special in the league. Coach Noll [former Pittsburgh Steelers head coach Chuck Noll, Dungy's first NFL boss] had always said to err on the side of production over looks, and Warrick certainly put that philosophy to the test. At just five feet eight and 180 pounds, Warrick was small for Florida State, let alone the pros. I double-checked my impressions with Bobby Bowden, and he told me that despite his size, Warrick was the best player he'd *ever* coached at Florida State. Coming from Coach Bowden, that was quite a compliment.

"Warrick had made many big plays for the Seminoles, and we desperately needed such a playmaker. In addition, Warrick was the kind of guy who would do other things that might not always be noticed by the fans. He picked up blitzes without fear, even if it meant blocking much bigger players. He had soft hands and caught the ball well coming out of the backfield. We didn't know whether Warrick could hold up physically for an entire season as the every-down running back, but *he* believed he could."

Dunn recognizes the huge opportunity afforded him by Dungy. If ever a mutual admiration society existed, these two are it. Asked about his old coach, Dunn feels the bar is raised when Dungy's name is mentioned, not just in relation to business on the field, but off it as well.

"He challenged me," Dunn says of Dungy. "He challenged me not just to be a good football player but to be a great person. I just think that if he hadn't challenged me as a rookie, would I be doing this today? You never know."

After being the Bucs' No. 1 pick with the twelfth overall selection of the '97 draft, Dunn moved his brothers and sisters to Tampa, his new place of employment. Busy, busy, busy would best describe Dunn in those days, playing father to his brothers and sisters, attentively looking after them in almost everything they did, in addition to learning his new assignments with the Buccaneers. Years later, the toll those responsibilities had taken on him were the impetus for Dunn seeking counseling. The process has helped him deal with the plethora of emotions evoked by the trauma of his mother's murder and the subsequent role he assumed as provider and father figure for his siblings.

"Dunn's subsequent life wasn't comparable to that of most pro athletes," notes SI.com writer Jeffri Chadiha, in his "Inside the NFL—Carrying a load: Therapy helps Warrick Dunn put the pieces together" [April 5, 2005]. "While his teammates went to clubs and parties after practice, Dunn went home to make sure his siblings had done their homework, cleaned their rooms, and eaten a home-cooked meal. What hasn't been mentioned much is the toll that caring for his family took on him. Friends and relatives say he often looked depressed in his early years with the Bucs. They remember him being guarded, closed off and overly concerned about the smallest of details. Dunn wasn't even aware of his somber moods until a Falcons teammate encouraged him to seek counseling in 2002."

The therapy came in handy in a way that Dunn at one time couldn't possibly have imagined. During a *Monday Night Football* telecast of an Atlanta-New Orleans game in early December 2007, a sidelines reporter for ESPN mentioned that Dunn was taking an unusual and courageous step to deal with his mother's murder that might finally put the horrific incident to rest. Through arrangements made by his attorneys, Dunn met with one of his mother's assailants in hopes of discovering more about the heinous occurrence that still haunts him fifteen years later. Interestingly, Dunn learned more about himself. Nationwide viewers were surprised to learn that he had no compelling desire to exact retribution on the man. It was a glimpse at the compassion that resides at the core of Warrick Dunn. To borrow a scouting combine term, Dunn, then, in humaneness, has a high vertical.

He is the man who turns up all over Tampa Bay, Atlanta, and two other cities benevolently assisting single parents in the dream quest for home ownership. Never far away is his deepest inspiration.

"I wanted to create a program to honor my mother's dream of owning her own home," Dunn says about Homes for the Holidays. "Providing down-payment assistance is really helping provide a 'hand up' to hardworking single parents."

As you might suspect, Dunn has been well recognized for his good heart and outstanding contributions in serving others. In 2004, he was honored with the Walter Payton NFL Man of the Year Award, the prestigious league honor that salutes community service as well as excellence on the field. Most recently, in January 2008, Dunn was named The Home Depot's inaugural NFL Neighborhood MVP for his humanitarianism. Other distinguished citations include the Giants Steps Award presented by former

President Bill Clinton in 1997, the NFL Extra Effort Award (1998), and an "Oprah's Angel" selection by Oprah Winfrey in 2001. He has been listed as one of *The Sporting News'* Top 100 most powerful sports personalities, made the same publication's 75 Good Guys in Sports list (1999, 2000, 2003, 2004), and in 2003 was ranked No. 79 on *Sports Illustrated*'s list of the 101 Most Influential Minorities in Sports.

To get a truer idea of what takes place when Dunn does his munificent thing, we accompanied him on November 13, 2007, a day on which the big-hearted athlete got to play Santa Claus to *four* new homeowners.

Chapter Thirteen

First Quarter
– 8:30 a.m.

Early morning sunlight shines directly into the eyes of three dozen people entering a small cul de sac off a country road in Canton, Georgia, less than an hour north of Atlanta. The front yard of the object of the people's attention—a town house with beige-colored siding on the far left-hand side of the cul de sac—is ensconced in shadow; early morning dew still evident on the tips of the newly sodded grass. An air of expectancy connects those present—representatives of the Cherokee County Habitat for Humanity, Woodmont Ladies Golf Association, Warrick Dunn Foundation, WDF sponsors, media, and the family of new homeowner Melanie Keith.

What draws the media is not the fact that another Habitat for Humanity home is being given away. They have come because a celebrity is there: Dunn. But the luminary is not looking for attention. He would be happier if this were all low profile, because it is not in his nature to try to bring notice to himself, particularly for his benevolent endeavors during the fall holidays and in the late spring around Mother's Day.

Dunn's goal is to surprise qualified single-parent first-time home buyers with down-payment assistance and a completely furnished home. Make no mistake about it, it *is* a surprise, and many people go to extraordinary lengths to see that it remains so, right up until the time the new homeowner walks in the front door.

"We've just about got it down to a science now," Natalie Boe, executive director of the Warrick Dunn Foundation, says of the philanthropic process undertaken by Dunn and his sponsors. "Warrick founded the foundation his rookie year with the Tampa Bay Buccaneers, in 1997. We've been fortunate enough to have supporters. He himself has been supporting the foundation."

Dunn indeed has dug substantially into his own pockets to see his dream become reality. Early on, he was the sole supplier of assistance, initially putting out $300,000 to propel Homes for the Holidays. Today, 95 percent of the Dunn Foundation's financial burden is carried by fundraising efforts and private donors, with 93 percent of all funds going directly into program costs.

"He's very involved," says Boe. "Here we are, eleven years later: seventy homes, as of now, and 182 children have been housed, including this morning's edition. By the end of today, that number will be 188 children, with seventy-three single moms." By the end of 2007, the figures would close at seventy-four single parents and 192 children and dependents aided.

As is the case with all homes involving the Warrick Dunn Foundation, buyers are kept in the dark about the extra assistance coming their way. Secrecy is instrumental in the role that Dunn and his foundation play. Not until two weeks before the official presentation is it revealed that they will be a part of the big day when the buyer takes possession. Family members are asked to maintain strict silence about the foundation's involvement right up to the time the new owner unlocks the front door and sees what's on the other side.

What's on the other side is Christmas in November, a cornucopia of plenty, a house come to life via a myriad of kindnesses breathed into it by Dunn and his handful of sponsors. That's Dunn's big payoff. He gets to be the host of a *Queen for a Day* scenario, where prizes and giveaways are the order of the hour. You almost expect him to pull back a big curtain to reveal what's behind Door No. 3—"Show her what she's won, Bill!"

Melanie Keith is no different than the other sixty-nine previous homeowners—usually single moms—who have benefited from the helping hand provided by the Warrick Dunn Foundation: She's in shock. "I can't believe my sister kept it from me!" she howls. But soon the inevitable tears of gratitude begin to choke her comments: "From the bottom of my heart—and Xavier's [Melanie's twelve-year-old son]—we really do appreciate it."

The element of keeping the Dunn Foundation's involvement a surprise from Keith was no small task for Cherokee County Habitat for Humanity Area Director Rita Arena.

"In a community where these women all know each other, I was afraid someone was going to start asking questions," recalls Arena. "I devised all kinds of stories, you have no idea. I called her dad, and spoke with him and told him that he *must* keep this a secret or it would ruin everything. It *has* to be a surprise, because I didn't know how else to get her out of work and Xavier out of school; that was quite a feat. So, I told Melanie she had to come for a walk-through before her closing, and that the only time the builder could do it was at eight thirty that morning. To compound it, her dad said that he had to take Melanie to the attorney's office that same morning at nine thirty, because the grandfather was going to prepare a will. Both her and her son were in the will, so Xavier had to get out of school so he could sign the papers. That was a way to get them all there without her knowing what was going on. Her dad, though, said, 'Make this walk-through fast, because she's got to get to the will signing on time.'

"It just worked out so well. Melanie was just so totally unaware of what we were doing. She had no idea of what was going to happen. This was my first time working with the Warrick Dunn Foundation. I don't know how they worked it; they were *wonderful* to work with."

Opening speeches in front of the home initiate the house opening. Warrick Dunn Foundation Board President Chris Knopik, who pitched in earlier by helping vacuum Melanie's new home, opens the ceremonies on this chilly morning speaking into a portable P.A. system set up just to the side of the front door.

"We have a lot of people who make a day like this happen," Knopik tells the small group clustered outside. "We have people who provide money, we have people who provide all sorts of things that go into a new home, and we have lots of volunteers who come together to make this day happen. We know that we've been working hard, Melanie, because *you've* been working hard to make this all happen for yourself and for Xavier."

Knopik invokes the names of Aaron's Sales & Lease, Frigidaire, and Night Vision—the Dunn Foundation's vital sponsors, who contribute to the outfitting of the dwelling. "This is our eleventh year offering assistance to first-time single-parent homeowners in helping them achieve their dream of home ownership; really, the American Dream," he continues. "We know, from keeping track of all our moms and families whom we have assisted over the years, that home ownership and the American Dream *is* a dream. It makes it happen. We see that this is part of the glue that holds families together—a stable, safe home, a place that is yours," he says to Keith.

Melanie's grandfather, Otis Keith, is asked to give a blessing. "I give thanks to God and all those who were involved in this. Thank you, thank you, thank everybody," says Keith, eighty, married fifty-nine years to his wife, Bertha. "It's a wonderful day. There's another stone in your crown when you go before the Cross," he says to any and all.

Canton Mayor Cecil Pruitt then stands before the assemblage and incants how "special people make special things happen. A gentleman who has earthly treasures who is certainly willing to lay up heavenly treasures, and all of you who have given your time to help people, that's what it's all about. I commend you and congratulate you, and I'm so grateful and proud to be a part of this beautiful city."

Of Dunn, he states: "This is a very special human being, as you know. I've followed his career from the time he refused to go to the University of Alabama to go to Florida State [peals of laughter arise from those in attendance]. I love him and appreciate him, and it broke my heart when that happened [more laughter], but it speaks for itself. All-American, all-everything; just a very special, special human being. Mr. Dunn, thank you for all that you do for this entire nation, brother. You're a very special example."

Dunn, dressed in black trousers, olive T-shirt, and black leather jacket, then addresses the gathering: "Good morning, good morning, good morning," he says in welcome, before eliciting laughter with, "I paid him for those words." A sincere tone of appreciation exudes from Dunn, as he thanks all who work with him. His regard for what Melanie has undertaken is unmistakable.

"I want to thank everyone who worked on the home," he says. "Aaron's—I love you guys. You've stuck by me ever since I moved to Atlanta. It's been an honor. Really. Just for me to be here is an honor. For all the things that I've been through in my life . . . losing my mom. Having trials and tribulations helps you understand life, it helps you appreciate the things that you have. What it teaches you is to open up your heart, to give back, to help other people live better. Today, I just am honored with the blessing of Melanie and her new home. I hope she enjoys it, and I hope you, Xavier, love it. I hope you guys really understand what this means to me. So, Melanie, congratulations. Here's the keys to your new home."

Melanie's makeover

If you've ever seen the reactions on the faces of real people who are the chosen beneficiaries on a show like *Extreme Makeover: Home Edition*, then you have an idea of what Melanie Keith experienced when she walked through the front door to her new home that November morning. A transformation takes place. People previously burdened by the weight of inescapable economic plight are immediately elevated to a new level of living. The effect is empowering. But before that realization hits, a sweeping wave of emotion hits the recipients head-on.

"Ohhhhhhhhhh!"

Upon entering her brand-new, beautifully appointed living room, Melanie bursts into joyful laughter, immediately followed by convulsive sobbing. Long pauses play out as she exhales silently through her tears. When Dunn steps forward to embrace her, she renews her weeping. It is a moving moment.

Dunn asks, "Whatcha think?"

"Oh, it's beautiful! Thank you!" Melanie manages between sobs.

Dunn, in the fine tradition of the game-show host, is quick to let her know there's more: "Let's walk into the next room. We've still got a lot of work to do."

Melanie gasps out another "Ohhhhh." Dunn assists her. "Do you want to start upstairs first?" But the woman isn't ready for that yet. Her whole body looks weak, like she'd rather sit down for a moment. She doesn't answer Dunn directly but simply continues to breathe heavily, the way people do when they're finishing a good cry. She is trying to deal with the enormity of what has just happened: entering her new home, a Habitat for Humanity home partnered with the Warrick Dunn Foundation and other contributors who have grandly set her up in her new residence with Xavier.

"Ohhhhh, thank you!" she says again, her voice barely audible.

Warrick Dunn tries out the couch in the new Habitat home of Melanie Keith and son Xavier.

"Let's start over here," Dunn says. "Let's check out this kitchen." The room has been stockpiled, cupboards and refrigerator overflowing with provisions. Melanie looks like she could use a respirator, her energy now almost totally drained by the magnitude of emotion emitted.

Others mosey about the room: Melanie's father, plus grandparents Otis and Bertha Keith and friends of the family. Of Melanie's grandmother, Bertha, Arena says, "She was so sweet. When we were inside she said to me, 'I'm so happy I lived for this day. She so deserves it.' I'm sure they have been concerned about her and the little boy."

The father, Wayne, was certainly no stranger to the project. "Her dad was there every Saturday in 105-degree heat, helping out," says Arena in awe. "And then her sisters and brothers, I mean they were really very supportive."

The sweat-equity clause is the crux of the Habitat for Humanity process. The organization's prospective first-time homeowners must put in three hundred hours of personal toil on the house, including help from family and friends, and no less than fifty hours themselves. Arena mentions that the "First Nail" ceremony took place on August 11, 2007.

"That's a celebration at which all the volunteers gather at the home site with the family," explains Arena. "They drive the first nail into the framing as an official dedication to the opening of the project. It is so emotional, I can't tell you."

The homes, then, are on a fast track to completion, generally finishing in less than two months. Melanie, born and raised in Canton, began her application process back in 2005.

"My goal was to be a homeowner, and my grandmother saw [the announcement] in the newspaper," says Keith, a machine operator for eighteen years with automotive parts manufacturer Piolax in Canton. "She said Habitat was accepting applications for housing. I went and got my application, and when I grabbed that application from that woman, I said, 'I am claiming it now. God is going to give me a house.' I was on the list about six months after I filled out my application. I had a home visit from the people from Habitat, and then six months after that they called and told me I was accepted."

For Habitat's part, Rita says: "We have a family application meeting, where the applicants are given all the information as far as what they have to do. They have to earn a certain income; they can't be under or over that amount. There's a lot involved in the processing. Once that's all completed, we move forward."

Meanwhile, the Warrick Dunn Foundation gift moves forward in the Keith home.

"What do you think, Xavier, you like it?" asks Boe, of Melanie's twelve-year-old son. The boy nods his head approvingly, dumbstruck by the enormity of what is taking place before him.

Of course, there's official business to attend to. Melanie signs the papers to her new house and also an indemnity sheet exempting

Dunn from any future liability in the event of a left turn in the Keith family's fortunes, or as he puts it, "so you can't come after me for anything." Laughs erupt all around, as Dunn is the last person in the room that Keith would likely "come after." A group photo follows with Dunn and the Keith family. "This may be on the Falcons Web site," says the star running back then with Atlanta.

Next, Dunn produces the big surprise for Melanie: a down payment of $5,000 on the new house, courtesy of the Warrick Dunn Foundation. "You can't keep the check," says Dunn, kidding her. "No, it's all yours. And if anything happens to the furniture, the people at Aaron's will take care of it."

Melanie laughs with the Habitat members about the lengths undertaken by all to keep her housewarming a secret. She is asked what went through her mind when she pulled up to the home that morning and saw all the people gathered there.

"I thought I was coming to do a walk-through," she says. "And I pulled up, and I'm thinking, *Why are all these people standing out here?* I got out of my car and was walking around and still I was like, *What are all these people doing here?* Then I saw him [Dunn], but after I saw him I still really didn't know why he was there. I was like, *I still don't know what is going on!*"

Melanie had heard of the NFL star, but just barely. "I know he played football and that sort of thing, and I knew he had an organization, but like, I was just in shock," she says. "I still really didn't know." Afterward, though, she had a more representative view of Dunn, the person. "He is just a blessing," she says. "For him to do that out of the kindness of his heart to help single moms out 'cause it is a struggle, I know it came from his heart, for him to just go out and do that. And he doesn't ask for no recognition, he just wants to do it out of the kindness of his heart."

Three days later, Melanie Keith is still in reverie. She is asked about Xavier's reaction, now that all the gratuities of the Dunn bestowal have had time to sink in.

"He has been telling everybody, 'I met Warrick Dunn! He has been at my house and gave us some stuff. I got a picture of him in my room!'" recalls Keith happily. "He is just excited about it and he loves that computer, 'cause he really did need one. I was going to get him one for Christmas, but ooohh, that is a blessing that took something off my shoulder."

Chapter Fourteen

SECOND QUARTER – 11:00 A.M.

On a quiet side street in the town of Sugar Hill, Georgia, Warrick Dunn greets the car that has carried Tiffany Miles, her daughter and son, and her brother to their new home.

At this second stop of the day, Dunn is immediately recognized, for Miles watches football. "I know you!" she says as she emerges from the auto.

Dunn seems to be genuinely and pleasantly surprised. "You do?" he says, flashing a big smile.

Later, she elaborates, "I saw him. I have seen him help others, and I had seen him on TV. I already knew about his foundation and what happened to his mother and everything like that."

Just barely above a whisper, Dunn says to her, "We're going to go inside your new house and check it out." Tiffany blurts an "okay" that barely beats a rush of tears.

"You all right? You excited?" Dunn asks warmly. "Don't cry yet, don't cry yet."

The running back places his hand affectionately on Tiffany's shoulder and leads her toward the front yard of her new home, where again, the small P.A. system has been set up for the opening ceremonies. As before, the Warrick Dunn Foundation's Chris Knopik emcees. To Tiffany, he says, "This is a great day for you. Some people would say that this is the first step for you, but we know, Tiffany, that you have been working and working and working for this day. It is our pleasure to be here with all of our partners—everyone—who help so much with what goes into a day like this, to give you a hand and help you along the way a little bit."

It is the second time that the WDF has partnered in a jumpstart for a new homeowner in Gwinnett County. "Tiffany and her family will not realize—believe me, I can say it in words, but they will not realize—what a great partner Aaron's is until they walk into their new home," Knopik says. After citing the Atlanta Women's Club for their assistance, he continues, "This is, for the Warrick Dunn Foundation, a wonderful year. We have just completed ten years of presenting homes to first-time homeowners and single-parent families. Earlier today, we did Home Number Seventy. This is Home Number Seventy-one. I know one thing: You can talk about numbers all day long, but the most important thing is that this is Home Number One." The remark elicits a round of applause.

"[This is one of] the most wonderful things I get to do," he adds. "When you're working on a board with a great organization like this, people say to me, 'Isn't it great to be able to work with people at Habitat, to meet Warrick Dunn, and work with him?' And I say, 'It really is.' But let me tell you what the highlight is. The highlight is this right here," exclaims Knopik with the skill of a ringmaster, turning to Tiffany Miles and her family.

A football fan, Knopik alerts the crowd to a milestone looming for his boss. "You may not keep up with these things the way that I do, because I'm an avid Warrick Dunn fan," he says, "but fifty-eight yards this Sunday, and he joins a very elite and very small group of running backs in NFL history who have gained 10,000 rushing yards." Enthusiastic applause erupts. "That's a big darn deal,"

Knopik asserts, before continuing. "People ask me, 'What's it like to know Warrick Dunn?' Warrick is exactly as you see him. He is a wonderful, caring guy, a shy guy who just gets up here and gives of himself, and . . ."

At this point, Dunn reaches into his pocket, extracts a handful of bills, and extends them toward Knopik. The gathering roars in delight. Knopik surges on. "He tells me privately that the most important thing he does is not on the football field; it's right here. We are so blessed to have Warrick Dunn."

Dunn, reserved as usual, takes his place in front of the microphone. "I have done a lot of things on the football field," he says, reiterating Knopik's previous comment, "but this is what life is all about. We're all blessed with a lot of gifts at different times, but when we're able to step back a little bit and help other people live that American Dream of owning a home, it's really an honor. For myself, having to go through a tragedy in my life, of my mom not having an opportunity to ever own a home, I felt like it was important that I present the opportunity to single parents. This is our seventy-first home that we've partnered, and though I'm excited, hopefully, to get 10,000 yards, this is the true joy of my life. I just want to say to Tiffany, 'Thank you.' She already knows about the program, so, that's okay. She's going to be really surprised."

Dunn turns to her. "I hope you really enjoy the home." With that, he pulls a set of house keys from his pocket and hands them to Miles. A happy cheer goes up from all.

Through building tears, Tiffany speaks hesitantly. "I just want to say thank-you to everybody. This is truly a blessing, a blessing and a new start." The tears pour now. "Thank you so much!"

"You speechless?"

Tiffany is escorted into the house by Dunn. She is speechless. Her eyes wander around the living room, glazed. It is too much to absorb.

"This is yours," Dunn says to Tiffany's five-year-old son, Jaiden, motioning to the sprawling living room couch. "You can sit on it; it's yours!"

A new computer gleams in the corner of the room. A Habitat docent takes Jaiden by the hand and leads him to his own room down the hallway. It is a situation the young child has never experienced; he has always shared a bedroom with others. Inside, the room is appointed with a bed, dresser, bed table, bookcase, and various toys sure to rivet Jaiden's attention, including current-fad Spider-Man gear. His eyes say what his voice cannot. Before long, he is immersed in the new gifts. Dunn takes time to play with him. An official NFL football, still in the box, rests atop the dresser. Someone suggests that Dunn sign the ball. He shyly shrugs, as if to say, "Sure, why not." A silver Sharpie is extended to him for the signing, but the pen is not up to the task. A substitute is summoned and performs ably.

Down the hallway, the mother spots a gorgeous desk in her ten-year-old daughter's new room. Her breath is taken away. "It's your desk!" The little girl goes over and runs her hand across the smooth surface. You can tell she doesn't quite know what to make of it, like maybe it will all vanish as soon as she leaves the room. Dunn continues to reassure her that it is hers.

"You speechless?" he asks. The girl shyly nods. "That's for homework, for HOMEWORK," Dunn instructs with mock sternness. Tianna moves from point to point in the room, examining her new treasures like a shopper after a big day at the mall. "That's your favorite color, pink, right?" asks Dunn. "See how smart we are? C'mon, we got some more house."

As the tour moves farther down the hallway, Tiffany lingers in her daughter's room. The little girl has excitedly drawn her mother's attention to the feel of the pink drapes that complement the color scheme of her room. "Ooooh, nice!" coos Tiffany. In the hall, Dunn introduces her to Rona Nasiri, Tiffany's new next-door neighbor, who has stepped in to observe the big hour. But the two already know each other, Rona having watched the Miles family work on the house for months.

Tiffany shares a common experience with Nasiri. In a geographic oddity, both are recipients of the Dunn Foundation's altruism with their new homes. Asked about her experience exactly one year ago, when she was the recipient of the Homes for the Holidays benevolence, Nasiri, who speaks little English, managed, "Surprised. I go to inside. See the surprise. Too much crying."

Too much crying. In a nutshell, that is the guaranteed emotional response from the grateful people benefiting from Dunn's caring. The question lingers like an echo: What triggers that part of a smallish, athletic kid to open his heart to the physical size of a city? In fact, several different cities, since his Homes for the Holidays program is additionally administered in Tampa, his hometown of Baton Rouge, and now in Tallahassee, home of Dunn's alma mater, where in December 2007, the program for the first time helped a single father and his family move into their own home.

Growin' up fast, he had said. And now his mom had become pure inspiration. *I wanted to create a program to honor my mother's dream.*

Tiffany is finally shown her room. A comfortable robe lies across the bed, and a pair of slippers wait on the floor. She canvasses her own private digs. "Ohhh, this is nice. This is nice, this is very nice!"

Billy, Tiffany's seventeen-year-old brother, will be living in the new home with his sister and her two children. Down the hall, he goes over his neatly appointed room. A picture of Dunn rests on a shelf.

"What's a picture of me doing there? It's not a girl or nothing like that," Dunn quips to the young man. "Speechless?"

"Always," replies Billy.

The Gwinnett County Habitat for Humanity president has been talking with Billy. "I asked him if he's texted his friends about what's been happening," the man says, "and he said he hasn't had time yet."

Dunn looks at Billy, now fidgeting with his cell phone, and determines that things are about to change. "Well, he's about to get on it, I can tell you that." Laughter fills the room.

Apparently Billy's wrestling coach has already called the young-ster to ask why he isn't in school that day, suggesting that he might have to pick up Billy every day to make sure he gets to school. Again, more laughter at the retelling of that episode. Billy, a senior at Suwanee's Peachtree Ridge High School, is asked his thoughts and feelings on the day to this point:

"It's been a blessing, to tell the truth," he says in a quiet voice. "I never would have expected something like this to come out of the whole thing. From the start till now, with helping out with other people's houses, and then to come to our own—it's been a blessing."

Miles says he has plans to join either the Air Force or Army fol-lowing graduation in 2008.

Leading the parade onward like a grand marshal, Dunn sug-gests, "Let's check out the kitchen." It seems the biggest oohs and ahs are reserved for this room. Squeals of delight escape from Tiffany, as she views the house's new ingestion center.

"Thought you'd like to eat," says the impish Dunn. As is the WDF custom, the kitchen is fully stocked. A pie sits at the center of a brand-new kitchen table, a reminder of the bounteous provisions stashed in cupboards and inside the new refrigerator. Tianna has dis-covered the goods are not just kitchen essentials: "Cookies!"

"You guys like it?" Dunn asks.

This time the bashful Miles children are more forthcoming. "Yeah," says little Jaiden.

Now, sounding like the portentous ghost of Christmas present, Dunn intones, "We're not done," and leads them to the back door. Out on the back step sits a new lawnmower plus a supporting cast of lawncare items. After a quick look-see, Dunn herds the party back to the kitchen table.

"C'mon in. You ready to sign the papers?"

Tiffany is only too happy to oblige. The pinnacle moment—the laying out of a $5,000 down payment on the Miles house—is about to unfold. Dunn crisply tears the check from its stub and hands it over to Tiffany.

"So, tomorrow you can hand it over at the closing, or give it now to these people right here," he says, nodding to one of the Gwinnett County Habitat for Humanity people. "Whenever you're ready," says the Habitat rep, who notes that the Miles house was built by Thrivent for Lutherans, a nonprofit that helps families achieve homeownership, and which, in this instance, has partnered with Habitat of Gwinnett.

Earlier, before Tiffany's arrival at the house, Beth Stubbings, director of development for Gwinnett County Habitat, talked about Miles and the new circumstances that will surround her.

"Tiffany was living with three other family members in a very small apartment, and those kids didn't have a yard to play in or any space to call their own, nor did she," notes Stubbings. "She's got a huge heart. She has made an effort, which is a tremendous effort for anybody who is fully employed, to come out on Saturdays and work 350 hours [along with family and friends] in her spare time. They attend financial planning classes—we're going to give them every chance to make it a success, because home ownership in this country really unlocks a lot of potential for the future.

"She can also borrow against the value of her home to send her kids to school," she continues. "It just unlocks so many financial opportunities and the chance to have all the things that a child needs—the same schools, the same friends, the same neighborhood—and none of the anxiety: Are they going to raise the rent? Can I *make* the rent? Is the landlord going to fix this? Is it safe for my kids? And this is hers from now on."

Stubbings then spoke of economic factors at play in Gwinnett County. "We have homeowners on the waiting list every year," she says. "These are people who make between twenty-five and fifty percent of the average income in Gwinnett County, and that's anywhere from $18,000 a year to $35,000, which really is not enough to get a person into a home in Gwinnett County. We partner with families who have the economic need and who meet economic criteria, but who also meet the need criteria. It's an interest-free mortgage, and almost inevitably, I have yet to encounter a situation where the monthly payment is anywhere like the rent you'd pay in Gwinnett County. A small apartment is a thousand dollars here. This house is going to be more like five hundred a month. The Warrick Dunn Foundation supplies the loving details. I'm just so impressed with what they do."

The woman then spots Dunn entering the new home prior to Miles's arrival. She gives him a heartfelt greeting: "What a beautiful, beautiful thing this is. Thank you," Stubbings says. "It's just such an unbelievable gift."

It turns out that Tiffany initially discovered Habitat online. "I found out from their Web site about this program that helps single families with a need," recalls Miles. "So I went to apply. I applied a couple of years ago and didn't qualify. I didn't make enough hours, or something like that. That was when I first got here that I tried. You have to work, I believe, thirty hours a week or so."

Tiffany, never married and from a broken home herself, had moved to the Atlanta area seven years ago from Phoenix, Arizona, where she had birthed her daughter, Tianna.

"You know I prayed and everything, and I just tried again," Miles says, regarding Habitat's application process. "My mom said, 'Don't give up, try again.' So last year I tried again, and I got through. They come up to your house to see if you have a need, and my need was my brother. I am a single mother; I took my brother in. I took him in and I have two children; they had to share a room and the same bed. That was my need."

The "need" element for Tiffany, though, began long before that.

"Our father, he's been incarcerated for most of Billy's life. He has been in there about seventeen years," says Miles, adding, "He has been in there since Billy was born."

Eight months earlier, in March 2007, Billy saw his father "for the first time in a long time," according to his sister. "I think he saw him when he was three years old."

It hasn't been much easier on Tiffany's children. Abandonment by the father is clearly an issue. Tiffany acknowledges that her kids ask about their dads, but sadly, there is little framework on which to build a further relationship.

"My son's father, he is here in Atlanta, but he just—I don't know, he just doesn't do what he needs to do," says Tiffany of Jaiden's dad. "He just does whatever he feels like. And my daughter's father is in Arizona. He doesn't do anything. He doesn't call her; he doesn't do anything. He has really abandoned. But Jaiden's father, he is around. He picks up his son every other weekend, but he doesn't do like he should. He doesn't buy any clothes, stuff like that; just when he gets ready, basically."

Having also experienced a life without a father, Tiffany finds herself being protective of younger brother Billy. "I'm trying to keep him on the right path, because I don't want to see him like that [in prison]," says Miles. "So many kids that age, especially teenagers, are getting in trouble, especially young black men. They just go another way."

Several days after the ceremonies, Tiffany is still on Cloud 9. "That describes it," she admits. "I thank God. I thank God because I want better for my children. I want them to have what we didn't have and encourage them, to let them know that it is important—the family and everything—and I want them to know that they are loved, and that if they don't have anybody else, they have their mom and they have God. Just have faith and believe. And that is what has happened. Because I've prayed every day, and I pray to God, and he answered my prayers."

Tianna and Jaiden also have had a little time to digest the changes in their lives wrought by the crusading efforts of Dunn et al. Miles expresses the newfound joy in her family.

"My daughter says it is like a dream for her," Tiffany says. "She says she just can't believe it. She is *so* excited about her desk, her own room, her own bed. And my son just keeps saying, 'I love this house, I love this house.' Now when I pick them up from school, they are like, 'Are we going to our new house? Are we going to our new house?' They tell all their friends about it. On the first day I picked them up from school, we didn't close that day. My daughter said, 'Can we just go into the house and just look at it?'"

The young girl didn't have to wait long. "I just closed yesterday," Tiffany said three days after the display of the Dunn Foundation benevolence. "My kids begged me. We haven't put all of our clothes over here or anything yet. They begged me, 'Can we please go to our house?' Why not?"

Indeed. The premises were ripe for beginning a new life; the house was hers. Tiffany had the paperwork to prove it. Asked where the event ranked in her life, she didn't hesitate to name it the best thing that had ever happened to her.

"This is, man, this is a dream come true. I still can't believe it."

She then paused to reflect on the wizard behind the curtain, the magician who pulled a house out of a hat. It was difficult not to think of Dunn, this windfall catalyst, as anything less than a knight in shining armor, a male hero she'd been waiting to see all her life.

"Really, he's really just a genuine person," Tiffany says. "You can tell he has a good heart, and not just by what he is doing. He is very soft spoken. You can just tell he is a good, good person. It's great that he doesn't forget. He doesn't forget about other people, how hard it was for his mother. That he gives back the way he does, that is God and his mother raising him right."

When someone is the recipient of a beautiful gift in the way Tiffany experienced on that unforgettable day in mid-November 2007, the result is a resounding gratefulness. One could never pay it back, but one could always pay it forward. Thoughts, for Tiffany, now lean toward the greater good of helping others.

"This experience is so wonderful, because I loved helping other people with their houses, and I know when my kids get of age where they are allowed to help, we are going to all go out as a family and help other people on their houses."

Dunn will no doubt be proud.

Chapter Fifteen

———

THIRD QUARTER
– 1:30 P.M.

Oh my God! Lord have mercy! Jesus Christ!"Jacquelyn Williams has opened the door to her new home and taken her first step inside. The Dunn Foundation cornucopia of plenty greets her.

"Oh, oh, goodness! Thank you all so much! We've been prayin', we have been prayin'." Jacquelyn's words become enmeshed with her outflow of tears and the gasps of breath between sobs. The emotion is so electric, so raw and genuine, that it seems at once a delight and an intrusion to witness. No lottery winner has ever shown more spontaneous happiness, outright joy, and heartfelt gratitude at an instantaneous change in personal fortune.

For Williams, such a bounty is difficult to comprehend. She is no stranger to hardship, having grown up one of twelve kids in her family, her mother pregnant nineteen times.

"Like I tell people all the time: Through that experience I learned how to care about others other than myself," says Williams, an Atlanta native who attended Fulton High before graduating from Price High School, "because growing up I never knew whether we was rich or poor. It's just that we always seemed to have everything we needed."

Those tough conditions spawned an awareness that armed Williams for a lifetime of selfless giving.

"To hear my mother say, 'Take care of that because you got to pass it on to your sisters,' that's how I learned to take care of my things, 'cause I knew somebody behind me would be gettin' 'em. I took care of whatever it was. That's how I grew up, learning how to care, putting a value on things. Right from the beginning."

Jacquelyn is called Grandma Williams because she gained legal custody of her daughter's two boys in order to raise them, after shuttling them endlessly between her daughter's place and her own home—an exercise in frustration and wear-and-tear for all involved.

"My daughter, she was working crazy shifts," Williams says. "She works at the Sheriff's Department in Clayton County, works at the jail. I was leery of anybody just keeping them at night, because after 9/11, she went to night shifts. She was just passing the boys about—this person keeping them, that person keeping them—and I told her, 'This can't work.' So, when I would leave my job at night, I would go to her house and watch the kids. Then I had to go to work the next day, so when she got home that morning, I would have to come way back to my house, back and forth.

"Then the price of gas is what really did it," she continues. "Gas went up so high, and I was like, 'We can't do this right here. We just need to let the kids come stay with me.' All the summers, they would stay with me, the whole summer, and I would take them home when school was in session, so I told her, 'This is just getting hectic, trying to rotate back and forth every night, on those cold nights.' I said, 'Look, just tell them to come stay with me.'"

The musical-chairs-with-the-kids craziness played out over a three-year span, Williams says. Now they're with her full time.

In her windshield, a major life marker—fifty years—looms. When younger, Jacquelyn Williams had harbored a dream of owning her own home by the time she was fifty. As events turned out, she beat the clock by two months. The path to her dream home had been clear-cut in Williams's mind for some time. She remembers not wanting to rush into it, of wanting to be able to procure her home without problems, "without no hectic." It had to be a home that she wanted. Then Williams, a resident of Section 8 housing the previous thirteen years, ran smack head-on into destiny.

"I was at a Section Eight meeting—they were having a seminar—and a lady stood up from Habitat," recalls Williams. "She was talking about this, that, and the other, and then she mentioned, 'You can become a homeowner.' Previously it's always been somebody helping you pay your rent, but I guess I never thought past that, to think that I could be buying my own home. I never thought that. I just always felt, 'Okay, somebody's helping me pay my rent, so it's good.' But this woman talked about owning your own home. I was like, 'You know something? That *is* something I would love to do!' So I took her little card and I called her; she sent me the information and I started from there. They told me everything, what to do. Everything just fell in place."

Shannon Sanders, communications manager for Atlanta Habitat, says the agency tries to place its prospective homeowners in a good situation from where they can be educated. "We make sure they're ready financially, and if they're not, they can come back," says Sanders. "Just because they get declined the first time—many of them that are in homes right now got declined the first time, and we said, 'Okay, you've got to go back and work on this and this and this. Then come back and reapply.' They get that straightened up, they come back, and they get in. We try to screen them well to make them successful. We don't want them to get in and not be successful or put them under undo stress anymore than they need.

"So, we get them in a good situation and educate them. Through us, through our affiliate—not all affiliates have it—but we have an education program. The qualifying homeowners take home maintenance classes, budgeting classes—we have several different kinds of financial classes—and they're required to do that; that's part of their sweat equity. They do sweat equity and education classes for a year. We've incorporated to make it bigger, so there's also some enjoyable, fun classes. We have our required budget classes, but they can also take landscaping classes, gardening-type classes, decorating classes, small remodeling projects, how to do things inexpensively, how to purchase in your community, how to get involved in the schools, how to make a difference through community involvement to teach them about local government—that kind of thing. I've sat in on a couple of classes and learned all kinds of things!"

Williams, a custodian for the past eight years at the city-owned Dunbar Neighborhood Center in Atlanta's Pittsburgh community, says she earns enough at her job to make the house payments. "I have nice benefits," she says, "but the greatest thing is, I make enough today to buy a home. I just didn't know that I was ready until I went to the seminar. You hear the least little thing and you're like, 'Okay, that sounds good.' You know? 'Cause I was really afraid. I'd been hearing my friends talking about escrow, and I said, 'I don't understand all that kind of stuff.' You hear, 'You gotta borrow from this bank, this lender'—it was just all sounding crazy to me. So I went to these little classes trying to learn what they meant by 'the percentage of this, that, and the other.' When I went to the Habitat thing, they made it simple, and I was able to understand. They said all you gotta do is pay this and fill out these forms, and I said, 'Okay.' They kept it simple."

Jacquelyn started out as a receptionist with the city only to find that more physical work better agreed with her. "I had been doing that for five years," she says. "We had a young man doing the floors, and he was retiring. I said, 'You know something? I want his job.' Because his job consists of climbing ladders, changing lightbulbs, walking around cleaning paper out of the yard, mostly a lot of physical stuff. I had been a fitness instructor for about twenty-something years. Just sitting there [as a receptionist], I was always tired; my eyes started hurting sitting in front of a computer all day. So now, I had bursitis in my shoulder. For about four years, I had taken everything for my shoulder to stop hurting; back and forth to the doctors. They were giving me steroid shots. I was just in pain all the time.

"When I took this floor tech job, they said, 'You're gonna have to be mopping every night. You're gonna have to be cleaning the bathrooms.' My friends were like, 'You mean to tell me you gonna take off your suit to be cleaning up bathrooms?' I said, 'I'm gonna try to be the best bathroom cleaner-upper you can be! If it means me being physical, if it means me being flexible, if it means me getting up and moving about, up and down, then that's what I need to be doing. If it means it's gonna make my health better, that's the job for me.' And I love my job."

Williams's inspirational attitude is her elixir for life's ills, job-related or otherwise. "It's the best medicine I could have received," she says. "The way I feel now, you cannot get it in a pill, you can't swallow it, you can't drink it. It has got to be a lifestyle. My health has always been number one in my life."

Specifically, Jacquelyn and her grandsons will be occupying a Hab Two home, meaning it was already constructed and the previous tenant had moved out, a rarity in the world of Habitat homes.

"They talk about the Hab Two program," says Williams. "I asked them, 'Well, what is that?' and they said it's when you can choose a house that's already been built. I had seen a house in a neighborhood that had been empty for about five years. And I told them, 'You know, that house is just sitting there. I'd rather have that house and fix it up.' And they said, 'Okay, we do those.' So we went to the property and I said, 'Look, I could fix this up and I could do this, that, and the other'—the house is like ten years old—so she said, 'I have to show you a second property,' because they show you two. So when she brought me to this property, she said, 'Well, this property here is twenty-five dollars a month more and it's got an extra room and an extra bathroom. You can choose whichever one you want.' I said, 'Oh my God. You mean to tell me I can get that one?' and she said, 'Yes, the lady's moving out of it.' I just said, 'Okay, let me catch my breath. I will take this one.'"

Williams, who does volunteer hours for Habitat, had been working in the neighborhood for a month but never knew the house she would ultimately live in was available. As things turned out, Williams believes a little Divine Providence figured in the mix.

"Yes, yes. Exactly," she says, before quickly adding that patience may have played an even bigger role. "I tell people all the time, 'This is a result of just waiting and waiting and waiting.' And that's what I did. I just waited patiently. I wanted to get something on my own. I had been married, been in domestic violence relationships, survived all of that, and I just wanted to wait patiently and get my home for me and my kids. That's what I did. I didn't want to rush out and just jump into something I couldn't afford or be trying to get something I couldn't keep. I said, 'Lord, I'm just gonna sit and wait patiently until it's my season. And I know You're gonna bring forth all my fruit.' And that's exactly what happened. And I mean it happened exactly that way."

That the house Jacquelyn was interested in became available is fairly uncommon. With Habitat mortgages relatively inexpensive (generally $600 a month or less) compared to going rent rates, and of course, with the loans being interest free, the default ratio is relatively low.

"I think we've had just fourteen in twenty-four years," says Habitat's Sanders. "Some, for whatever reason, have had to move away. Habitat for Humanity gets the first right of refusal on the home to buy it back. Some of them say, 'We want you to buy it back; we *want* this to go to another family.' Some have invested for quite a long time, which means they get a higher percentage of the money the longer they've been in their home. They can't sell their homes, and of course, the longer they've been in there the more they've invested. After fifteen years, they're fully invested, and then they can sell it. Not many do. But when they do, we've had a few who've come back and said, 'It doesn't matter on the price.' They want the market value, but they're like, 'We want to make sure this house goes back into the program.' They don't want it to just go out to the general public, because they were so fortunate to have this experience. Yeah, it's kind of neat that we have homeowners who want the house to go back, but we don't do that a whole lot either."

Williams, in her unfailing belief that her house would arrive in due time in accordance with God's plan for her, started packing.

"It was this year, around the middle of May," she recalls. "And I mean it all happened so quickly. I was in another house. I started packing last year in December. I had made my mind up: By this December I will be in my own home. I will not rent anymore. Being on Section Eight, when I was working a part-time job, my rent was only $300. But when I started looking at full-time jobs, I would've ended up paying almost $700. So I was like, 'No, uh-uh, it's time for me to start buying.'"

It became Williams's definition of faith and her nonverbal call to arms.

"Exactly. I mean . . . *exactly.*"

She moved forward, not knowing how it would all work out but knowing that it *would* work out.

"That's exactly what I did. All my friends are like, 'Girl, are you still packing?' I'd be like, 'You know something? The day will come, but until then I'm gonna wait patiently—and all my stuff will be ready.' And that is exactly how it happened."

Outside, Chris Knopik acknowledges Williams's big heart in his opening remarks to the family members, friends, Habitat people, and media spread out on the front lawn that slopes down to a quiet dirt road. It is only minutes before Jacquelyn enters her new home, and as he has done at the two previous stops today, Knopik plays Ed McMahon to Dunn's Saint Nick. This particular Habitat dwelling lies in southeast Atlanta—one of 941 homes built by the organization in the city.

"We salute you on the hard work that went into the making of your dream—to own a home by the time you got to that magical age," says Knopik. The Atlanta executive director of Habitat for Humanity is then brought up for a few words.

Dunn formally addresses the group, as he has at the two earlier ceremonies, with self-effacement and humility. "Obviously, this is very close and dear to me," he begins, "because my mother lost her life and my grandmother embraced us as a family, particularly my five brothers and sisters. It's really an honor," he says, looking at Williams, "to see that you're doing the same thing. For someone to give up their life and their time to raise their grandkids, to me, that's just huge. The work that she's done over the years to get to this point, I commend her for doing that. Today is really an honor.

"I've been blessed, obviously, but to me, this is the true blessing in life. Home ownership is important. I know I'm close to 10,000 yards, but I've been running my whole life. A couple more yards, that's okay, but this is something my heart lives for—Homes for the Holidays. So, Mrs. Williams—Grandma Williams—congratulations."

Jacquelyn steps before the mike. She has heard the speeches by those before her, and she now knows that something pretty spectacular is happening, although she's just not sure what. Like the new homeowners earlier, she is miffed at the turnout.

"I was like, 'I know that is the house, so why are all those people standing there?'" she says. "'Why are all those people in the yard?'"

Her address is short and sincere. "Everybody, thank you. This is one of the most joyous days of my life. Thank you all. Thank you, thank you." More words of gratitude and the shameless shedding of tears will follow shortly, when she is shown inside. Dunn then thanks his corps of sponsors before admitting to the crowd, "I can't wait till we open that door!"

"All you have to do is bring your clothes"

Following Williams's invocation of the Almighty and her heartfelt exclamation of joy, thanks, and tears, Dunn, ever the calming voice in the torrent of swirling feelings in front of him, reassures her that this is only the beginning.

"Let's get you started," he says. "I want you to see the living room." Jacquelyn, her two grandsons in tow, goes over to touch the sofa, like it might vanish into thin air if she didn't feel it first.

"This is all yours," says Dunn soothingly. "You like it? You gotta take care of it, though, right?" he says in the direction of eleven-year-old Joele Fanning, Williams's elder grandson. The boy wordlessly nods his head, beyond shy in the presence of so many strangers and the unfamiliar glare of television cameras. Accountability is a small but important part of Dunn's presentation when kids are involved, and he never misses a chance to give a learning lesson to a fatherless child. In this case, the boys' stewardship of the home and its contents is a critical element in the mix. Though these newfound possessions may be gifts from a famous and benevolent source, their upkeep is as important as the imparting of the gifts themselves.

The procession heads towards the kitchen. "This is so all grandmothers can cook," Dunn says, gesturing toward the new appliances.

In amazement, Williams clasps her hands across her chest. "Oh, *definitely!*"

"I'm sure you won't have a problem eating," Dunn continues, before opening the food-crammed cupboards.

"Can't you tell?" Williams says with a chuckle. As the cupboards and the refrigerator door are opened, she screams: "Oh, my goodness! Yes!"

They move down the hallway, first stopping at Joele's bedroom on the right. "Oh, guys, come this way! Look!" Jacquelyn says, tearing again. Inside, besides what one might expect to find in the way of furnishings in an adolescent's room, a brand-new computer sits atop a desk, beckoning to the eleven-year-old.

"You like it?" asks Dunn of the boy. "It's yours!"

Down the hall from the older boy's room, eight-year-old Xavier's new digs are shown. He is quiet. "You camera shy right now?" asks Dunn. The child's room, as with the previous houses, is stocked with toys—but not just any toys. In this case, Xavier, Joele, and their grandmother love to camp, so tents are part of the gift—another personal touch of the Dunn Foundation, which researches the interests of its beneficiaries. It seems, in this instance, that the foundation beat Williams to the punch.

"I was telling them every year I would buy them a tent," says Jacquelyn, "because boys like doing stuff. My father always let my brothers build stuff. Kids have to learn how to do stuff with their hands. Like, my boys have always had a dog. My father always had dogs. I have always had a dog. We *still* have a dog right now. To me, giving a child a pet teaches them how to take care of someone other than themselves. They've got to feed them, they've got to do this and that and the other. But the tent, it is adventurous. It is so much fun.

"When they were very young," she says, "I bought them a tent and a flashlight, 'cause they were afraid of the dark. We would go outside and put the tent up, and I would make popcorn and sandwiches. I was like, 'Look guys we are out here for eight hours. You can't go in the house, so everything we need we've got to take outside.' So that is what we would do. Then they'd be like, 'Grandma, it's getting dark' and I would say, 'We got our flashlight.' It teaches them not to be afraid of the dark. Them knowing they got their flashlight makes them feel safe."

Williams was hoping they'd get to bivouac before bad weather hits. "Yeah, it is about to get cold, but I told them before it gets cold we will have a chance to put the tent up right on the side of the house," she says. "There are things you can do around the house without leaving the house. I ain't got to drive two hundred miles to go camping when I can go right in my backyard. Paradise is in your mind, you know."

The room-to-room procession continues. "We're not done yet," pipes Dunn. "You guys mind washcloths?" He leads the family into a hall bathroom. It is fully appointed with all the necessities. "We got to make sure it's done *right*."

If Williams felt she was emotionally spent by this time, she learned how deep the well of feelings can go, as Dunn silently shows her into her own bedroom. In a rising crescendo, Williams roars out at the very top of her lungs: "Ohhhhh, my goodness … YES! YES! This is *my* room!" The emotion is broken by laughter as a spectator underscores the woman's new level of privacy: "Don't come in *he-uh!*"

She comes upon a discovery: "A walk-in closet!" Williams now is reduced to a stream of consecutive thank-yous, punctuated by more gleeful cackles and a series of yeses, ordinary words failing her. This last bit of excitement leaves the woman trying to catch her breath. It is obviously something beyond her prayers and wildest dreams.

Suddenly, the smacking sound of an impact resounds just outside the woman's bedroom. An official NFL football, one of the gifts in Xavier's room, has been unboxed and its content rocketed through the trailing entourage, caroming off the hallway wall.

Once more Dunn instantly and skillfully translates an event into a life lesson. "Put the ball down!" he commands to the boys in a no-nonsense tone. "No ball playing in the house! No ball playing in the house!" As with Jaiden and Tianna Miles and Xavier Keith, the day's earlier recipients, the Williams grandkids have grown up without benefit of a male presence in the home.

"Their father's in prison," shares Jacquelyn. "Every now and then their mother was taking them to see him, but like I tell her, that's just not a place that kids need to be going. Whatever happened,

happened. I'd just rather they didn't go, so we did that in the best interests of the kids."

One senses that Dunn's mini-lecture is a relatively foreign experience for the boys: a behavior edict emanating from an adult male. The ball tossing quickly ceases.

"They knew it," Williams later says of the incident. "Kids have got to be taught. We think our children know because of who we are; no they don't, they've got to be taught. It takes a man to teach a young boy how to be a man. It takes a man's voice to make a young man act differently."

Williams continues expressing amazement at her new world. Fresh new towels in a basket catch her eye in her personal bathroom. "It's just beautiful, just beautiful," she says, shaking her head.

"All you have to do is bring your clothes," offers Dunn. "That's it."

"That's the blessed part," Jacquelyn says, slowly repeating Dunn's words. "Just bring my clothes. I am *so* excited." She is introduced to other Warrick Dunn Foundation members, before Dunn shows her yet another set of gifts—a lawnmower and auxiliary outdoor accoutrements, all of which will come in handy for Williams, an avid gardener.

"I thought all women like to do that," Williams says of her favorite pastime. "I went to the store once and bought three tomatoes, and it was almost four dollars. I said this is the last time Publix gets this money. I can grow a tomato! So I left there and went to Home Depot and bought a tomato plant. I love plants. I have had plants all my life. My mother used to say, 'You buy real plants and see them grow and see how your life expands.' Artificial plants, they just sit still. They don't do anything. They just sit, whereas with a live plant you can see the growth. It's like a relationship, when two people plant a seed and take care of it. If you want an apple orchard, you've got to plant a seed. You won't be pulling apples the next week. It's not like that. Relationships are like seeds: You got to watch it grow and nothing grows it but time."

It's evident that patience has played a major role in Williams's life, her struggles punctuated by the presence of an unshakable faith and enough down-home wisdom to take on the fiercest tides. Now, with the bounteous bestowal of the Dunn Foundation gifts, she will again reunite with all things green and growing.

Standing in the doorframe to the backyard, Dunn intones for the boys' benefit, "Y'all gotta get to work." It's additional subtle encouragement aimed at shaping their concept of responsibility. The woman gives Dunn a final hug combined with a flurry of thank-yous, as more tears find their way to her cheeks. The obligatory paperwork and the final gift of the down payment from Dunn complete the proceedings.

Later, on the front veranda, Dunn is approached for comments by the media. In his soft-toned, laconic way, the running back answers questions from a Fox 5 News reporter and explains how well Williams fits the Homes for the Holidays program.

"She had to do a lot of work just to get to this point—community service, lining up credit, qualifying for the loan," says Dunn of Williams's undertaking with Habitat. "She had to take financial classes, maintain a regular job—in all, just doing a lot of stuff that, when you work hard, you're rewarded. This is like a beginning. This is *not* a handout, where she doesn't have to do anything as a parent. They have to go out and *maintain*. Instead of paying rent, she has a mortgage. Now she's getting equity in the home. There's a lot of benefits to what Habitat for Humanity has done over the years, and she's just the next recipient that has benefited from that."

He is asked his feelings, knowing that Grandma Williams is doing exactly what Dunn's grandmother had done in caring for him and his siblings fifteen years before.

"I don't know if this is the second or third grandmother, but we had one last year, in Tampa, and she had ten grandkids," notes

Dunn. "To sacrifice so much and take on her ten grandkids, to work so hard to provide for them, to me, it's a life. Grandma Williams is doing the same thing. She's sacrificing a lot, but she's very deserving. This was her dream—home ownership. Just to have the opportunity to be a part of that, for me, is an honor."

Her coworkers call Williams the "givingest" individual they know and say the Dunn conferral couldn't have happened to a better person.

"The best part is knowing I can help out at a particular moment," says Williams of assisting others. "At work one day a girl came in. She didn't have a belt on. I said, 'Where's your belt?' and she said, 'I forgot it.' I said, 'Look, I got on a uniform. Take mine.' And she said, 'Ms. Jackie, I . . .' I said, 'Honey, it's just a belt.'

"You have to put people before anything else, and everything will work out," she continues. "Whenever you put anything before people, it is a problem, so I don't put nothing before people. Nothing. Sometimes a person just might need a 'Good morning, how you doing?' I never ask a person if anything is wrong. I say, 'Is everything okay?' I learned how to put positiveness in people's lives, and it don't cost a dime. My mother used to say, 'A kind word don't cost a penny.' My mother taught me if you can't say something nice, don't open your mouth. And that is where I'm at in my life. If I can't say kind words, I don't say anything.

"Focusing on positive thoughts, it is just healthier. It takes the *same* amount of energy to do right as it does to do wrong. The same amount. It's just that when you walk straight, you do right. My mother, she would give us something to do like cleaning the bathroom. If you didn't do it right the first time, she made you clean the bathroom *and* the kitchen. I knew if I did something, I had to do it right the first time, or my mother would be hollering at me, making me do it over again."

Those substantive lessons, hard-earned on the front end, are the backbone of Williams's belief system and her approach to raising her own grandchildren now.

"I was the same way with my kids," Jacquelyn says of parenting. "My sister would say, 'You too hard on them, I feel sorry for them.' You don't have to be their friend. I am their mother. We have to be parents. Today, parents are trying to get their children to be their friends. Let them find friends in school. You have to be stronger than their friends are going to be. We are not going to put them in a car and go flying around the curve going a hundred miles an hour. People who you think are your friends will do that to you. I am a parent. I tell them all the time: I am a certified grandparent now."

It would seem a bright future beckons for Xavier and Joele, their course along life's path much encouraged by their grandmother's principle-driven tutelage, and now, there's the boost from Dunn. As the list of Homes for the Holidays recipients grows longer, one wonders if it's possible to maintain what has been initiated with those who have been touched by the goodwill.

"We keep in contact with everybody; our foundation works to stay in touch with each family," Dunn says, leaving no doubts about his long-term commitment. "I still see a lot of similarities. Obviously, times have changed, situations change, but I see people who are working hard, who are doing everything they possibly can do to achieve that American dream. To be in the position I'm in to help these guys get there, that's the *least* I can do. It keeps me humble that there are a lot of great people who have worked hard, people who are not as blessed as I am. To come back into the community and help deliver that dream, it's a lot better than the game of football. *This* is my life, not football."

The television reporter then reminds Dunn that the Falcons' upcoming game gives him an opportunity to do something pretty special—to go over the 10,000-yard career rushing mark against his old team, Tampa Bay.

"I'm just going to go out and practice hard and just play, just run," Dunn says. "Like I've said before, I've been running all of my life, since I was seven. To have had the career I've had and to hopefully have the opportunity to be in that elite company [of 10,000-yard rushers], to me, it's what pays off from dedication. I've been fortunate. I love the game of football; I have a passion about it. I just hope I have that opportunity. If not, then, it'll come. When it happens, I'll be joyful and thankful."

Dunn's magnificence, both on and off the field, isn't lost on Williams. While she'd heard of Dunn as a fan, through his association with the Falcons, she confesses she knew little about the other side of the man, the compassionate giver.

"He is the greatest," Williams says without reservation. "I mean, he is a good guy. He is genuine. It was very heartwarming what he did. Me and the kids are just lovin' it, you know? It's just a great feeling to know that people care. So much is happening in the world right now, and it is just a wonderful blessing. He is my hero. I mean he is really a blessing. To move into a new home and it is already furnished? All I have got to do now is pay my mortgage. That's it."

She adds that there's no mistaking Dunn's genuineness. "It just came natural. The only thing that I knew about him was through the Falcons or reading an article in the paper about him. This was it. This was just it, and I can't even put it into words how great it felt."

Three days later, Grandma Williams was still pinching herself. "I am still trying to digest it," she says. "I'm gradually getting things straight. I had to go to the other house and get my clothes and stuff. Other than that, I am just at peace. Everything is just wonderful. Definitely it seemed like it was just a dream. It seems like I am still dreaming, like, *Is this really true? Did this really happen?*"

Life imitating dreams. And then there was the continuing wonder of it all for Xavier and Joele. "They are delighted," acknowledges Williams. "'Grandma, is this really ours? Grandma . . .' I was like, 'Yes, yes, we need to go to bed now.' It is like you lay down and they get up, 'Grandma?' and I'm like, 'Please lay down.' So, we were up early this morning, and they are in there asleep right now. We are just exhausted."

Thinking of the boys reminded me of something Joele had said in the midst of the mayhem celebration several days before. Joele, an articulate boy with a gift for succinctly stating the obvious, had seemed to put the afternoon's experience into the perfect perspective. Asked what he thought of all that had come down in the way of good fortune for him, his brother, and his grandmother that day, the eleven-year-old paused before replying thoughtfully, "Some things words can't explain."

Chapter Sixteen

FOURTH QUARTER
– 3:30 P.M.

This house was built all by women. It's called the Atlanta women's build," proudly states Atlanta Habitat for Humanity Communications Manager Shannon Sanders, as the Dunn Foundation caravan pulls up to its fourth and final home of the day, this one in southwest Atlanta. "Even our construction staff and our skilled supervisors, they're women as well." Chris Knopik adjusts his opening comments to reflect the all-women's effort. "They wanted to get it right!" he says to enthusiastic applause. "We've got to know our limitations, men. Our place is to say, 'Yes, ma'am,' sometimes."

A man named Marshall Thomas, a community liaison to the local District Four councilperson, is called upon to speak. In tow is a cute little boy sipping a soft drink from a cup—a grandson? He is a born scene-stealer. It's hard to look at him without smiling. Thomas ends his remarks with a guaranteed crowd-pleaser this day: "Women make the world go 'round."

Before the event, awaiting new homeowner Kia Savage to arrive, Dunn chats informally with a group of women somehow connected to the events of the afternoon. It is evident by their star-struck demeanor that they haven't met him before. Awe is in the air. One jolly woman hugs him, afterward letting out a loud "Hooeeeee!" followed by an exclamation to the effect that Dunn is one hunk of a man. Thomas, a bystander to the scene, comes forward with the ad-lib remark of the day:

"Now, you know, ladies," the community liaison chides good-naturedly, "in some circles that might be interpreted as a sexist remark!" Everyone in the near vicinity howls.

Knopik returns to introduce the new homeowner. In his remarks, he mentions that hard work is no stranger to Kia Savage, in that, during her collegiate days at Lincoln University in Pennsylvania, she had gained national track and field titles as a Division III school champion in the 55-meter dash and the 4x100-meter relay. The crowd standing on the sidewalk extends out onto the quiet street in front of the house. Collectively they stir at the athletic background divulged on Savage.

Her track accomplishments are one thing. How she even got there is another. A onetime student at Samuel S. Fels in Philadelphia, Savage didn't even run high school track, due to some untimely program cuts from the school budget. Women's track was one of them.

"All throughout junior high and high school I played basketball, because they didn't have track where I went to school. So I played basketball," recounts Savage. "Then I wanted to go to a school so I could run track, and when I got there that year it was cut out of the budget. So I didn't start running until I went to Lincoln University."

It was at Lincoln that Savage first realized she had talent for track. "I walked on, and in my first meet, my first indoor meet, I qualified for the nationals. I had no clue what the nationals were. I had no clue. I was the last one off the blocks and qualified going in with the fastest time in my whole division."

Though the sprints—the 55-meter, 200-meter, and 400-meter—were her specialties, Kia decided to try her hand at the grueling hill-and-dale style of long distance running known as cross-country. Generally, runners fall into one of two categories—sprinters or distance runners—and the twain rarely meet, except when sprinters are attempting to stay in shape in the off-season by doing a little distance work. Savage, though, found success in that discipline as well.

"I guess I got a little bit of the speed and distance, 'cause I also ran cross-country," she says. Turns out Savage made the nationals in that event, too.

The remembrance leads the woman to a contemporary development with her running. One she is pleased with. "I just actually ran not too long ago, last month [October '07], with Clark Atlanta [University], just to see where I was at," says Savage. "I hadn't run cross-country in about ten years. I wanted to see where I was at with the young girls, and I wound up coming in fourteenth place."

Savage clocked a time of 26:05 for the 3.2-mile course. "I thought that was pretty good for a thirty-one-year-old who's been off the field for a long time," she laughs. Still, the passion remains for running as the years begin to mount. While distance runners normally begin entering their prime at Kia's age, sprinters are generally in their late teens to mid-twenties. She figures she's got an uphill climb. But then, hardship is nothing new to Savage.

"It's in my system and my coaches are like, 'You know, you might as well give it up. You can always be a champion in something else,'" she says of her practically minded mentors. "But I really don't want to accept that right now. I want to ride it out. There were a lot of things that were keeping me back. I would go to work, then after work go straight to track practice. Mind you, I'd been on my feet for eight hours and I'm going straight to practice. That persisted for about two years, and I wasn't getting any therapy 'cause I didn't have sponsorships. Here I am, just a Division III champion trying to get to the Olympic Trials, and I was doing it all on my own out of sheer passion. But because of not having finances to get therapy, I met injury. I had a herniated disc from the weight room, and that put me out for a couple of months. Then I healed up and I was right back at it. I still met the same difficulty, with trying to work and train and be a mom. You can't do the three."

This is the toughness and the hard work that Knopik referenced earlier, the character-building experiences that fashion a person into who they eventually become. Overcoming athletic injuries is tough, but that was the least of Savage's hurdles when she first made her decision to move to Atlanta in her quest to train and hopefully qualify for the 2004 Olympic Trials.

"I had spoken with a coach who had sold me a pipe dream over the phone," begins Savage of her travails upon relocating to Atlanta in 2003 from her hometown of Philadelphia. "I was anxious and excited to find out that I'd be able to train without having to work. That's what got me down here, and it turned out to be something different. I was living with him, along with another athlete. At the time, my daughter was two, and she was still nursing. It got very strenuous. It was something different than what he had told me over the phone, and we had to find other living arrangements at the last moment. So I'm traveling around Atlanta, trying to figure out where we were going to stay."

The crisis involved many a night sleeping in her car. "That was a trial within itself," she says. "I had to send my daughter to South Carolina to live with my grandmother, because I didn't have a home. I had to figure out how I was gonna make it work with a thousand dollars. Fortunately, I had that much to work with. That was everything that I had, and I had to make that into something. I think I moved six or seven times within a two-month span."

It was then that a friend stepped forward with an encouraging suggestion. "A girlfriend of mine told me about Habitat, and I was so excited," says Kia. "She called and was like, 'Oh, but you have to be in a job for two years.'" Kia had to seek employment, eventually finding a job with Whole Foods Company as a cashier. "I love it, I love it," she says happily today. "I haven't tried to go anywhere since then. All the other departments have tried to get me into their department, but I just love the front end. That's where you interact with the customers one on one, and I really like people. I'm a people person."

Kia filled out her Habitat paperwork, keeping it organized in file folders before applying in April 2007. Her shift in fortune was about to begin. "I got approved instantly, and the ball got rolling very quickly," she says. "The first day of the home build was September fifteenth."

A family implant

"Our hats are off to you!" Chris Knopik says to Kia Savage in commendation, wrapping up his opening remarks.

Dunn is introduced for the final time this day. In his comments, to further identify with Savage, he brings up the fact that his deceased mother had run track in high school. "She was a state champion in the hurdles—a little correlation right there," he says, smiling, in reference to Kia's accomplishments on the cinders. "I understand the trials and tribulations that you've been through. Like Chris said, it's hard work to be a track athlete. You have to sacrifice things; you have to sacrifice your body. And she did that to become a champion, obviously. She's also worked hard at her life to get to this point. For me, it's really an honor just to help you. All the people here—Girl Scouts, Aaron's, Pepsi, Air Tram—all these sponsors today have helped get me this dream of helping others with home ownership. Congratulations."

Kia is asked to step to the microphone. She is still unaware of the fuss surrounding her new home. "When I saw the people I was like, 'Okay. What's going on?' But I still didn't have a clue. The ironic thing is I really didn't know who Warrick Dunn was prior to this, 'cause I'm not a football fanatic and I did not have cable for a number of months to really be tuned in. I believe I did hear about the foundation, but I still really didn't know who he was at the time."

The Dunn Foundation's concealment of its selection of Savage for special assistance was, like the previous three home presentations, well maintained. So when Kia was asked to address the throng outside her new home, she spoke only about what she knew at that moment: that the Habitat house was an incalculable lift to her life. Still, she had no idea of the surprises awaiting her inside.

"Wow, this is the best pre-Thanksgiving present I could have ever asked for," she says to the assembly. "I appreciate and thank all of you for this opportunity. We're definitely going to cherish it and take care of our little home and make sure we do everything we can to assist Habitat in building future homes for residents, like myself and my daughter. And thank you, Jenn, for booking my little cute house!"

"Jenn" is Jennifer Krix, a Habitat employee in her mid-twenties, and the foreman on the all-women's build. "This is my sixth house with Atlanta Habitat," she says of the thirty- to forty-strong volunteer womanpower behind the building effort. "It was really cool."

The house, unbelievably, was erected in seven Saturdays. "We got permits, got the house turned over, the punch work, painting—all with women, in seven Saturdays," notes Krix. "It was very cool, because it was very girl-powered and very empowering. This was my first women's build."

Krix knew that the house was destined for Savage even before construction began, because Habitat requires the new homeowner to be vested in so many sweat-equity hours.

"They're out here every Saturday," says Krix, "but I didn't know she was getting the Warrick Dunn until two weeks ago."

WARRICK DUNN FOUNDATION/DAVID WALTER BANKS

A thrilled Kia Savage gives Warrick Dunn a hug as they walk through her new abode, an Atlanta Habitat for Humanity home built entirely by women.

The masquerade needed to maintain the secrecy of getting "the Warrick Dunn" is a feat comparable to keeping a surprise party a surprise. As Rita Arena revealed earlier, relative to Melanie Keith's assistance from the Dunn Foundation, clandestine efforts by all involved are required if the big day is to remain a secret from the recipient.

"It was hard just trying to get Kia's daughter out of school and get Kia herself off from work and get her out of the house and find some reason why I had to pick her up, since she has her own car and could get here by herself," Krix confesses. "She lives not but a couple of miles from here. So we had to make up this whole thing about not coming to the house, and I'm really bad at that kind of thing."

To Krix's way of thinking, the Habitat concept is all about people like Kia Savage.

"I couldn't pick a better homeowner to deserve it," Krix says about Savage. "She has worked *so* hard on this house, and she was just in it every step of the way. It's great when you get a homeowner who's actually in it, who shakes hands with the volunteers in the morning and develops a relationship with the volunteers. Some of the women who were here at the dedication also helped build on the site, so they got to know Kia's daughter, and they know Kia's story. She was just in it. She would even come out and paint during the week when she got off work. We have developed a really good relationship. We call each other; sometimes it's about what's going on with the house, sometimes I'll call just to see how she's doing."

The all-woman crew experience was a first for Krix, a Habitat house leader for three years who formerly worked in marketing and accounting. The crew works from blueprints with architects, in addition to the contractors, who are their bosses. "But as far as Saturdays, when we have fifty-plus volunteers out on the site, it's pretty much, 'Here's fifty volunteers. Build a house,'" she says. "It goes beyond being a contractor or being a construction worker. As a house leader, you've got to be a people person; you have to learn how to micromanage and how to keep fifty people busy while being happy while getting stuff done all at the same time."

"They train you for six months before they give you your first house," she says of her work with Habitat. The event was such a delight, she said, that she will be doing it again—in the spring of 2008, in fact, with Marist High School. The women's build for Savage's home was independently sponsored by individual donors.

"It was just a bunch of women who wanted to donate their time and money, and help out on the house," says Krix, who enjoys a laugh when it is suggested that she participated in an all-women's version of TV's popular *Extreme Makeover.* "I had so much fun with the skill supervisors who were out on this site. A lot of good girl friends got to come out, and we all got to work together. I had no idea what I was getting into, and didn't know what to expect. It wound up being better than I ever could have imagined. And like I said, Kia more than anything deserves this award. It's just really cool."

As they did at the three previous homes, the media gather inside the house immediately on the other side of the front door to catch Kia's reaction as she and her six-year-old daughter, Ashayla Curry Quick, unlock the door and step inside.

"No words can really explain the emotions that I felt," recalls Savage. "I was in shock. I was overjoyed and extremely, extremely grateful. I just thought it was a wonderful, wonderful, wonderful gift. I almost felt like it was too much. I kept saying, 'It's too much! It's too much!' I'm the one who's always giving. I'll give my last when I don't even have it."

That heart of the giver often knows a reverse side. Those bestowing can be at a loss when on the receiving end.

"I always find that when people try to give me money, I'm like, 'No . . .' Even when I would need it I wouldn't accept it. I've never called my parents for anything. I'd be down here struggling, and I just worked hard to get it for myself."

Inside her new home, Savage and her daughter are given the *Queen for a Day* treatment by master of ceremonies Dunn. Especially fun is presenting her own bedroom to Ashayla.

"Wow, a pink room!" says the little girl.

"Whatcha think?" asks Dunn. "You like it?" The little girl nods approvingly. "It's yours. You can sit on it. It's YOURS!" Ashayla hesitantly sits on the edge of the bed, taking it all in.

Later, Kia reveals an ironic incident involving her daughter that borders on the clairvoyant.

"A couple of weeks ago I had found a picture that she drew last year of a huge house shaped like the house we have now," Savage recounts. "She was standing in front, and it showed someone in the top window, and I'm like, 'Shayla this is our house!' It was a drawing of the future. I kept it and I want to put it up."

Dunn now beckons the girl and her smiling mom, "C'mon, we got some more of the house to see."

Kia, a little more reserved than the other homeowners Dunn has assisted previously on the day, begins to tear up in the hallway between rooms. "This is making me cry," she says softly. Dunn is comforting in his response.

"Crying is good sometimes."

Ashayla runs up to her mother. "Mommy, look at your room!"

"Want to see mommy's room?" Dunn asks Kia. If he'd produced a magic wand, it couldn't have been more effective.

"Oh yeah, check it out."

Kia ratchets her feelings up a few notches when she sees the bounty lying within. Dunn, the comedian, walks over to a familiar looking object. "This is the best thing in this room, right? A picture of me."

It's all beginning to hit Kia. "Wowwwww!"

Dunn: "You like it?"

Savage begins to giggle.

"Feels good? Come on, we have some more house to see."

The kitchen, stocked of course, is next on the agenda. "Oh, my goodness!" says Kia at first sight. "This is too much!"

"You like to eat, huh?" asks Dunn kiddingly of Ashayla.

"Mmm-hmm," the little girl answers.

"Man!" says Savage, still in amazement at the array of appliances and consumer goods. "Oh, man!"

"It's yours," offers Dunn quietly.

The young girl is asked by both her mother and Dunn what she thinks.

"I like it," she says unhesitatingly. Dunn kids the girl, saying, "See this camera here? Jump up and down for Aaron's, saying, 'I like it! I like it!'"

The script runs the usual way the remainder of Savage's tour of the house: lawnmower, paperwork, intercut with endless, sincere thank-yous and Oh-my-Gods from the mother. Ashayla and her mom hug tightly after the papers are signed.

"Are you happy?" Kia asks her daughter. They both giggle in the embrace, shell-shocked by the altruism directed their way.

Dunn asks the little girl her favorite thing in the new home. Ashayla thinks a few seconds and decides that there's more than one favorite thing. "These two," she says, pointing toward the living room and kitchen area.

"One last thing," says Dunn, saving the down-payment assistance check for the grand finale. It elicits a tearful thanks from Kia. Ashayla, seeing her mother overcome, brings her a tissue. Kia sniffs and dabs her eyes, shaking quietly.

Several days later, Kia isn't the only one still in Neverland. "For a six-year-old, she's been showing me her character," she says of Ashayla. "She's always upbeat, but she's just been very, very, very excited and upbeat [since the house ceremonies]. We're still in transition. We haven't spent the night there yet. We're still in our apartment, but she went to school the next day and was telling the children and the faculty, "Finally we got a house!"

Savage rates the event the No. 1 thing to happen to her in her life. Well, almost. It seems there's a competitor, one that Dunn assuredly would gladly step aside for.

"This is the top," says Kia. "I told someone today, 'This is the best thing that's ever happened to me—other than meeting my father for the first time in my life when I was twenty-one.'"

There's more, with a bit of an O. Henry twist.

"I was under the impression that someone else was my father for a long time," notes Savage, "and he had passed away when I was seventeen. He had died of a heroin overdose, and that was a shock to me because I never knew he did drugs until the day of his death. Three or four years later, and here it is I find out I had *another* father, and I'm like, 'Wait, wait a minute! You mean I get a second chance on having a parent?' So I called him and he came right over, and come to find out his last name was Quick, and that made me Kid Quick."

An appropriate appellation, to be sure, for someone destined to be a national track champion. But the surprises don't end there. Kia's dad's first cousin is none other than former Philadelphia Eagles five-time Pro Bowler Mike Quick, a speedy wide receiver, who, in 1983—just his second season in the NFL—caught thirteen touchdown passes and led the entire league in receiving yards.

"I found that out after meeting my dad," says Savage, who logically concludes that the family gene pool touched her as well. "So that's where I get the athleticism from."

It's difficult to imagine the emotions Savage went through, one moment thinking that a chapter in her life was closed only to discover a new situation dawning, one accompanied by renewed possibilities.

"But it's been a roller-coaster," she adds. "Just this last year we found out that he has to go on dialysis, and he didn't even know his kidneys had failed. His knee started to swell up and he went to the doctor and that's how he found out. I was the only sibling that came forward to be tested for a kidney transplant. I told him that I would. He's like, 'I'm older'—because he's fifty-five—and I'm like, 'Well, you know, you still have so much more time left to share. I don't want you to go on me already.' We just really got introduced to each other."

Savage says the two were able to build bridges back together after a very, very long absence.

"Yes, immediately," she says. "I mean, we just got right to it. Funny thing is, me and him are closer than any of his children, than any of my other siblings."

It's nice to hear a story involving a father and a child reconnecting. The tale offers hope that it can occur elsewhere. But as Tony Dungy pointed out in his staggering finding—that two-thirds of African-American teens are currently being raised without a father in the home—it is nonetheless an uphill battle. Through the vehicle of his own trauma surrounding the premature death of his mother, Dunn quietly bonds with the single moms he helps. He knows firsthand the horrors of having to grab the spinning wheel of an out-of-control ship in a tumultuous storm, with passengers—family—aboard.

As pointed out in the earlier accounts of the new Habitat home-owners benefiting from the Dunn Foundation's benevolence, most of the fatherless children helped by Dunn and his sponsors have not known an empowering male presence in their lives. Thus far, that holds true for Kia's young daughter, who hasn't lived under the same roof with her father since she was a year old.

While reconstructing the relationship with her own dad has been an encouraging element in Savage's life, her current family, her new family, isn't far away.

"I was so amazed to walk into my house and see that, even though I don't have any family here, I have an implanted family that's actually thinking about me, that furnished my whole entire house."

❦❦❦ ❦❦❦ ❦❦❦

Having witnessed Dunn at his philanthropic best, one wonders at the man. He is so genuinely connected with the business of help-ing others, light years away from the stereotypically cool million-aire athlete paying lip service from the tinted glass of a limousine. I like the way one NFL community relations director put it about the real off-the-field heroes like Dunn: "He doesn't phone it in." His heart is so engaged in what he feels is his *real* calling. It's inspiring to observe.

"It's a very great program for single moms that he has put together," says Savage, of Homes for the Holidays. "It gives people the opportunity to know that there still is hope for all the hard work that you put out, that you still can be rewarded. It's comforting to know that someone is thinking about us in that way."

Dunn, of course, has been fortunate—or honored, as he puts it—to partake from the vantage point of the benefactor. "Each experience is unique because everyone's reaction is different," he says. "Each mom has her own way of expressing her gratitude, and it's always special. It is truly priceless."

The Homes undertaking has made such a positive impact that other notable NFL stars have been moved to join Dunn's cause. Arizona Cardinals quarterback Kurt Warner and ten-year Tampa Bay Buccaneers linebacker Sheldon Quarles have aligned with the Dunn Foundation, assisting single moms in their respective communities—Warner in Arizona and St. Louis, where he played prior to being traded to the New York Giants in 2004, and Quarles back in his hometown of Nashville.

"Guys just reach out, seeing how they can get involved or be a part of it," says Dunn of the efforts of Warner and Quarles. "A lot of guys want to go into their own communities and touch people. We've all grown up in similar situations and lived this life, so they can really relate to it. They're that much more passionate about it, helping people live their dream. Eventually, we would like to expand the program to every NFL city, working with our sponsors to help single-parent families achieve the dream of home ownership."

Outside, after the ceremonies at Savage's home, Dunn, who is used to the withering grind of four quarters of football, is tired, although not visibly. With these kinds of heart-warming experiences, it's not the physical activity that wears him out.

"This is the most I've done in one day," he says of his four-home marathon. "It takes quite a toll on the emotions."

Overtime – 11:00 p.m.

That night, I tune in Atlanta's eleven o'clock Fox 5 newscast to see what the local media have to say about the day we had all experienced, to relive those mini-miracles that had taken place at the four Habitat homes. Soon the wealth of good acts performed by the

Warrick Dunn Foundation and its sponsors that will forever change the lives of four single-parent families will be heralded as the wonderful deeds that they are.

If ever the point were made that good news doesn't sell—a contention many of us wish not to believe, like hearing that there's no Easter bunny—I soon witness that disturbing fact firsthand, and with repugnant dismay.

Finally, at the close of the hour-long broadcast, the Fox crew's film account begins. Dunn is standing on Grandma Williams's new veranda, the same location where I had held my own microphone alongside the reporter's. Dunn had been asked several questions about his altruism, the bounty bestowed on the new homeowner during the emotional presentation, Habitat, and the Homes for the Holidays program. Only the reporter's last question had pertained to football.

You can guess which part of the interview made it onto the news that night. It seems there was only time in the segment for one question and answer from Dunn, the gift-giver supreme—about the upcoming game on Sunday against his former team.

It is a sad commentary on our society that good news—important news—so often is shunted aside in favor of doom and gloom or the faddishly sensational. So on this particular occasion, as is so often the case, Dunn's beneficent deeds would remain mostly anonymous. Just the way he likes it.

PART FOUR

THEY ALSO SERVE

Chapter Seventeen

THEY ALSO SERVE

While it is impossible to acknowledge all the good deeds and philanthropic achievements of current or former NFL players, the following is an alphabetical presentation of twenty of the league's more prominent "givers" toward the betterment of the human condition. Complete lists of the Walter Payton NFL Man of the Year Award winners, the NFL Players Association's Byron "Whizzer" White Humanitarian Award recipients, and the Bart Starr Award honorees appear in the Appendix following the player philanthropy profiles below.

DREW BREES, *New Orleans Saints quarterback*

Since his arrival in the Crescent City, Brees and his Brees Dream Foundation have been hyperactive in the community, particularly in the wake of Hurricane Katrina. His "Cocktails for Katrina" fundraiser, not long after signing with the Saints in the spring of 2006, benefited the NFL's Youth Education Town (YET) and the rebuilding of a football facility used by several area high school teams. He and his foundation also launched "Brees on the Seas," an annual event that takes kids deep-sea fishing off the Louisiana coast. In June 2007, Brees and wife Brittany kicked off a drive to raise $2.5 million for the children of New Orleans, through their Operation Kids initiative. In addition, the couple hosts an annual charity golf tournament, the Professional Open, whose proceeds go to children's causes in New Orleans and San Diego, his former place of residence and employment, when he was with the Chargers. His foundation also helps fund programs with Purdue University, Brees' alma mater.

KEITH BROOKING, *Atlanta Falcons linebacker*

The five-time Pro Bowler has twice been named the Falcons' Walter Payton Man of the Year, in 2002 and 2006, for his extensive community involvement. He founded The Keith Brooking Children's Foundation in 2003 to serve foster children in metro Atlanta, an undertaking honoring his mother, who was a foster parent while Brooking was growing up. He also raises funds and collects food for the Atlanta Community Food Bank, donating fifty-six dollars—matching his jersey number—for every tackle he makes in a game. Brooking coordinates the annual Bird for a Bird turkey drive, preparing holiday meals with other Atlanta celebrities during the Great Thanksgiving Dish. In addition, he assists his old high school in East Coweta, Georgia, conducting a yearly off-season golf tournament to benefit the school's athletic department. In 2007, Brooking continued his efforts to serve foster children through a golf tournament fundraiser and a Tailgate Kick-Off fundraising event.

DERRICK BROOKS, *Tampa Bay Buccaneers linebacker*

A ten-time consecutive Pro Bowler and 2006 Pro Bowl MVP, Brooks has impacted the lives of thousands of Tampa Bay area youth through his Derrick Brooks Charities, founded in 1997. The charities' cornerstone program, the Brooks Bunch, serves youngsters from the Wilbert Davis, Ybor City, and Brandon Boys & Girls

Clubs and incorporates a classroom element, with panel presentation and behavior and grade assessments leading up to trips around the country and elsewhere. Brooks has accompanied his Bunch on college tours to New York, Chicago, and Tallahassee, as well as to Atlanta, Washington, D.C., and the western United States. In 2000 and 2005, program members earning their way traveled with the nine-time All-Pro to South Africa to visit Johannesburg and Cape Town, among other places. Brooks's community involvement also includes annual Thanksgiving dinner distributions and a holiday party for underprivileged children. Brooks can claim the Big Three in NFL humanitarian awards: He's the 2000 Walter Payton NFL Man of the Year Award cowinner (with Chicago's Jim Flanigan) and the recipient of the 2004 Bart Starr and Byron "Whizzer" White awards.

KRIS BROWN, *Houston Texans kicker*

Brown has helped better two communities during his nine-year pro career, actively working with the Western Pennsylvania School for the Deaf and Junior Achievement's "Kickin' for Kids" program while in Pittsburgh as a Steeler for his first three NFL seasons. In 2003, his second year with the Houston Texans, Brown and his wife Amy founded Kris Brown's Kick Club, inspired by his sister April's courageous fight with a rare form of cancer at age eleven. She survived that attack, but the experience left Brown wanting to help families battling cancer. Whenever he scores a point during the regular season, Houston area corporate partners, along with the Browns, kick in $250 to the Kick Club. In 2007, Brown totaled the second-highest point total of his career, 115. The Club has raised more than $475,000 for the Texas Children's Hospital Charity Care Program, which financially assists families in need.

KEITH BULLUCK, *Tennessee Titans linebacker*

So solid have been Bulluck's contributions to the Mid-South that, in 2007, the outstanding two-time All-Pro was voted the team's Walter Payton Man of the Year winner for the second consecutive year. As a former foster child, Bulluck, knowing the many difficulties in life to be overcome by foster kids, founded The Keith Bulluck Believe & Achieve Foundation in 2003 to benefit foster care children. Through his programs, Bulluck provides educational and financial assistance to participants through such events as his annual Wine and Roses Wine Tasting and Auction and his yearly Halloween party for more than a hundred children. He also hosts a Spring Bling Bowling Day for fifty boys from the Department of Children Services, My Friend's House, and Youth Villages. In addition, in 2006, his foundation partnered with New Horizons to benefit young adults seventeen to twenty-one in obtaining computer network technology training. In 2007, for the second straight year, Bulluck served as spokesperson for National Foster Care Month.

Nate Clements, San Francisco 49ers cornerback

It was a noteworthy first year in a new city for the onetime Ohio State star. On the field, Clements and linebacker Patrick Willis were named the 49ers' Bill Walsh Award winners as team co-MVPs. Since joining San Francisco prior to the 2007 season, Clements, a former Buffalo Bills Pro Bowl defensive back, has helped build a home in San Jose with Habitat for Humanity, assisted in beautifying a park in San Francisco's Bayview district, provided Halloween costumes for students with good attendance, and hosted children on a holiday shopping spree. For his service, the 49ers selected him as their 2007 Walter Payton Man of the Year Award recipient. Inspired by an aunt suffering from leukemia, Clements is donating the $1,000 prize from the honor to his hometown Leukemia & Lymphoma Society in Cleveland, Ohio.

Trent Dilfer, thirteen-year NFL quarterback

A quarterback for five NFL teams over his thirteen-year career, Dilfer established the TD 4 HIM Foundation in memory of his son

Trevin, who passed away from a rare heart disease in 2003. The foundation provides financial assistance for interdenominational ministries, various youth programs, the Boys & Girls Clubs, cancer research groups, and religious organizations. The Super Bowl XXXV champion quarterback is a multiple Walter Payton Man of the Year winner with two different teams: the 49ers in 2006 and the Seattle Seahawks in 2002. At Seattle, in 2003, teammates awarded him the Steve Largent Award, emblematic of the player who "best exemplifies the spirit, dedication, and integrity of the Seahawks." The proceeds from a 2006 Dilfer charity golf event yielded new artificial grass for his native Aptos (CA) High's football stadium.

DONALD DRIVER, *Green Bay Packers wide receiver*

Driver has made more than 315 charity and community-related appearances since being drafted by the Packers in 1999. With his wife, he created the Donald Driver Foundation in 2001 to offer assistance to single moms, sick children with weighty hospital bills, and to provide housing for the homeless and to address education issues. Recently, the foundation opened two computer labs in Houston, Texas, inner-city youth centers. In addition, Driver conducts two football camps, one each in Houston and Mississippi, and a golf tournament in Houston. He has been a frequent speaker at Green Bay-area schools and has made pediatric visits to St. Vincent Hospital in Green Bay, been involved with "Junior Power Pack"—the Packers' fan club for kids—local Pop Warner Football, and the Brown County Association for Retarded Citizens (now ASPIRO). For his altruistic contributions, Driver received the 2001 Community Service Award from the Green Bay Chamber of Commerce, the Professional Achievement Award at the Lee Remmel Sports Award Banquet in 2006, and was named the Packers' Walter Payton NFL Man of the Year in 2002.

BRIAN GRIESE, *Tampa Bay Buccaneers quarterback*

Through the Judith Ann Griese Foundation, established in 2001 in memory of his mother, Brian Griese began Judi's House in Denver, Colorado, a safe haven for grieving children and their families who have lost a loved one. Brian's mother died of breast cancer when he was twelve, and Griese endured a difficult time with the grieving process. Since November 2002, the facility he founded has served more than seventeen hundred children, teenagers, and their adult caregivers. Griese also conducts an annual golf tournament in Michigan to benefit C. S. Motts Children's Hospital and took part in the All Children's Hospital 2004 Fall Carnival for pediatric patients. Actively involved in fundraising efforts for the Susan G. Komen Breast Cancer Foundation, Griese served as honorary chairman for the 2001 Race for the Cure in Denver, and in 2002, served as honorary chairman for PUSH for the Cure, a fund-raising effort to benefit spinal cord and brain injury research at Denver's Craig Hospital.

JOHN LYNCH, *Denver Broncos safety*

Through his John Lynch Foundation, the nine-time Pro Bowler and 2007 Justice Byron R. "Whizzer" White Humanitarian Award winner honors outstanding local student-athletes through a variety of programs. He has been recognized as a three-time winner of the Walter Payton Man of the Year award on the team level, garnering the distinction in 2001 and '02 with Tampa Bay and in 2005 with Denver. In December 2007, Lynch and his wife, Linda, hosted their eleventh annual Christmas Party, at the Denver Center for the Performing Arts, during which thirty-five Denver-area kids were each given a hundred dollars' worth of toys. With brother-in-law John Allred, Lynch raised nearly one million dollars in the last five years through their annual celebrity golf tournament, which has resulted in a new Boys & Girls Clubs branch in San Diego. In 2006, Lynch was honored with the Bart Starr Award, voted on by NFL players, for his community benevolence, and in January 2007, received the Wooden Cup for the highest standards of character and citizenship.

Peyton Manning, *Indianapolis Colts quarterback*

Since 1999, Manning, the Walter Payton NFL Man of the Year in 2005, has hosted an annual flag football game at the Colts' practice facility that benefits children from CASA (Court Appointed Special Advocates), described by the court system as "guardian angels of abused and neglected kids." Manning was CASA national spokesman in 1998-99. His PeyBack Foundation sponsors "Taking Care of Those in Need," an annual Thanksgiving giveaway in Indianapolis, at which more than six hundred needy families receive a full Thanksgiving meal. The foundation also distributes fifty tickets to each home game to kids selected by local community organizations. His annual PeyBack Bowl in Indianapolis, a bowling event featuring Manning and other celebrities, raises money for at-risk youngsters in Indiana, Tennessee, and Louisiana. But in addition to his charities, a significant call to aid in 2005 earned Manning true hero status. Following Hurricane Katrina's catastrophic swath through his native New Orleans, and with younger brother Eli at his side, Manning got hold of a plane, helped fill it with 30,000 pounds of relief supplies, then flew to Louisiana to personally deliver the aid.

Deuce McAllister, *New Orleans Saints running back*

The 2006 *Sporting News* No. 1 Good Guy co-award winner, McAllister and his Catch 22 Foundation have been a dependable source for putting money and resources into the Gulf Coast region in the post-Katrina aftermath. He also is involved in aiding the New Orleans educational system and its football programs. "I've worked with public schools through my foundation, donating items, talking to the kids and trying to give them the materials to be successful," McAllister said in a 2007 article on TIME.com. "Whether they're sharing books or can't take books home because there aren't enough, you see how much they lack. Every school doesn't have that problem, but the majority do." McAllister also has his "Deuce-days," twice-a-month outings for local youth during the school year, in which members of area university sports teams donate their time to chaperone trips to museums, sporting events, and swamp tours, to name a few.

ROMAN OBEN, *San Diego Chargers offensive tackle*

The 2007 Big Brothers Big Sisters Man of the Year, Oben has been especially proactive in helping his native African homeland of Cameroon. Since 2004, through his West Africa Outreach, Oben and his foundation have worked to facilitate educational aid in Africa. Those efforts include funding overseas shipment of 230 computers used to complete the installation of the largest computer network in West Africa, plus the purchase of 195 textbooks and the payment of academic fees for sixty-five primary school children in Buea, the capital of Cameroon. With his help, a dormitory for HOTPEC—the Handicapped and Orphanage Training, Production and Ecstasy Centre, also in Buea—was completed. In 2003, Oben was honored by the Vincent T. Lombardi Foundation as a Vince Lombardi Champion for community service in Washington D.C., where he grew up after moving to the States when he was five. He also supports the United Way, Special Olympics, and the fight against illiteracy and hunger.

JASON TAYLOR, *Miami Dolphins defensive end*

Taylor, the NFL's 2007 Walter Payton Man of the Year Award winner, is the third Miami Dolphins player to be accorded the honor, joining Hall of Famers Dwight Stephenson (1985) and Dan Marino (1998). For the first time in the award's thirty-seven-year history, the winner was announced live on national television before the kickoff of Super Bowl XLII. In 2007, the Jason Taylor

Foundation chipped in nearly $320,000 to assist programs and organizations helping young people, including launching the Jason Taylor Reading Room in Miramar, Florida, an after-school program addressing illiteracy among inner-city youth. Taylor also contributed $50,000 to the Holtz Children's Hospital in Miami to support the Jason Taylor Children's Learning Center, a recreational and educational hub for hospitalized children. One of the foundation's more popular programs, started in 2005, is "Cool Gear for the School Year," in which disadvantaged kids get to shop at Old Navy for new school clothes.

LaDAINIAN TOMLINSON, *San Diego Chargers running back*

No stranger to celebrity for his on-field exploits, Tomlinson, the 2006 NFL MVP, garnered an equal accolade for altruism that same year, when he was named co-winner of the Walter Payton NFL Man of the Year Award along with New Orleans' Brees. To that impressive achievement he has also added the 2008 Bart Starr Award, named after the Green Bay Packers Hall of Famer, honoring Starr's lifelong commitment as a positive role model. Tomlinson and his Touching Lives Foundation, profiled on CBS's *60 Minutes* in December 2007, host youth football camps, a yearly charity golf tournament, present Christmas gifts for ill children, and issue annual scholarships to college-bound students. Just two days before Thanksgiving 2007, he supplied two thousand families with enough food to enjoy their own Thanksgiving dinner. In addition, the foundation hands out dozens of bikes and hundreds of shoes to underprivileged kids in San Diego.

HINES WARD, *Pittsburgh Steelers wide receiver*

Ward, a four-time Pro Bowl receiver, established the Hines Ward Helping Hands Foundation in 2006 to fight discrimination of biracial children in his native Korea, kicking it off with a $1 million donation of his own then raising another $1.5 million through corporate donations. In 2007, for the second year, Ward brought a group of Korean kids to Pittsburgh to join him as guests at a Steelers game. The biracial offspring of a Korean mother and African-American father, Ward, a 2007 Walter Payton NFL Man of the Year Award finalist, created the foundation in honor of his mother, Kim Young-He, who raised him as a single parent. Ward also co-hosts the Hoge/Starks/Ward golf outing that benefits the Caring Foundation and Caring Team, with team-mate Max Starks and former Steelers running back Merril Hoge. Proceeds benefit western Pennsylvania children and families struggling with the death of a parent or sibling.

KURT WARNER, *Arizona Cardinals quarterback*

With his wife Brenda, Warner, a two-time NFL MVP, created his First Things First Foundation in 2001 to promote Christian values and help those less fortunate, sponsoring trips to Disney World for sick children, building recreation centers in children's hospitals, helping single moms achieve the dream of home owner-ship—initially partnering with Tampa Bay's Warrick Dunn—and teaching Special Olympians football fundamentals. In addition, the Warners' foundation sponsors service-based mission traveling trips for high school and college-age groups. Warner's annual celebrity flag football tournament is an interesting concept, in which touch football teams from the corporate world compete in a two-day tournament. The teams are bolstered by the presence of former and current NFL players, in the pigskin equivalent of a pro-celeb golf tournament. In all, First Things First conducts no less than thirteen community programs.

BRIAN WATERS, *Kansas City Chiefs guard*

This eight-year veteran and 2007 finalist for the Walter Payton NFL Man of the Year Award began his Brian Waters 54 Foundation in 2005 to provide opportunities for underprivileged children and

families in his hometown of Waxahachie, Texas, as well as his place
of employment, Kansas City. Over a four-year period, Waters, a
three-time Pro Bowler, donated $100,000 to revitalize Waxa-
hachie's Pee Wee Football program. He volunteers regularly at The
Promise House in Dallas, which serves homeless, runaway, and at-
risk youth, and also co-chairs the Chiefs' offensive linemen in their
First Downs for Down Syndrome initiative, in addition to speaking
on behalf of the Chiefs for "Think Pink," a campaign for breast cancer research. "For Me," Waters has said, "the gridiron serves a
greater purpose."

ROY WILLIAMS, *Dallas Cowboys strong safety*

In July 2004, inspired by his sister Alecia's efforts as a single
mom to provide a better life for her young son, Williams, a five-time
Pro Bowler, launched the Roy Williams Safety Net Foundation to
help low-income single mothers in the Dallas area receive support
and assistance through a variety of programs, including partnering
with local community colleges and trade schools to offer scholarship
assistance to those single mothers wishing to pursue an education.
The Safety Net Foundation also sponsors an annual Healthy Homes
Day, working with area health agencies to provide screenings,
immunizations, and educational materials to low-income single
moms. In addition, Williams's foundation also directs the annual
holiday Gift of Giving toy drive, benefiting children of low-income
single moms who might otherwise not receive Christmas gifts. In
the five short years since its inception, Williams and his foundation
have helped the lives of more than three hundred single mothers
and their families.

JERRY WUNSCH, *former Tampa Bay/Seattle tackle-guard*

Each February for the past ten years, the former interior lineman for the Tampa Bay Buccaneers and Seattle Seahawks, along
with his wife, Melissa, has sponsored Circle of Friends Winter Week

for children with cancer and chronic blood disorders, a five-day ski trip to Jerry's hometown of Wausau, Wisconsin. The Wunsch Family Foundation was inspired by a cousin of Wunsch, who waged a courageous fight against cancer as a young mother before succumbing in 1997. Wunsch later partnered with former Seahawks defensive end Grant Wistrom in 2001, expanding the program to include children from other cities as far away as Tampa, Atlanta, and St. Louis. From their collective efforts, approximately fifty-five people now make the annual trip. In September 2007, Wunsch was selected Impact Player of the Year by the Board of Directors of NFL Charities, an honor identifying an exemplary NFL Player Foundation and its efforts to make a difference in the communities it serves.

NFL PLAYERS HONORED FOR COMMUNITY SERVICE

- Byron "Whizzer" White Humanitarian Award
- Walter Payton NFL Man of the Year Award
- Bart Starr Award

Byron "Whizzer" White
Humanitarian Award Winners

2007	John Lynch, Denver Broncos
2006	Steve McNair, Tennessee Titans
2005	Peyton Manning, Indianapolis Colts
2004	Derrick Brooks, Tampa Bay Buccaneers
2003	Troy Vincent, Philadelphia Eagles
2002	Mark Brunell, Jacksonville Jaguars
2001	Michael McCrary, Baltimore Ravens
2000	Doug Pelfrey, Cincinnati Bengals
1999	Cris Carter, Minnesota Vikings
1998	Hardy Nickerson, Tampa Bay Buccaneers
1997	Chris Zorich, Chicago Bears
1996	Bill Brooks, Buffalo Bills
1995	Derrick Thomas, Kansas City Chiefs
1994	Mark Kelso, Buffalo Bills
1993	Nick Lowery, Kansas City Chiefs
1992	Reggie White, Green Bay Packers
1991	Mike Kenn, Atlanta Falcons
1990	Ozzie Newsome, Cleveland Browns
1989	Mike Singletary, Chicago Bears
1988	Deron Cherry, Kansas City Chiefs
1987	George Martin, New York Giants
1986	Nat Moore, Miami Dolphins
1985	Reggie Williams, Cincinnati Bengals
1984	Rolf Benirschke, San Diego Chargers
1983	Doug Dieken, Cleveland Browns
1982	Franco Harris, Pittsburgh Steelers
1981	Ken Houston, Washington Redskins
1980	Gene Upshaw, Los Angeles Raiders
1979	Roger Staubach, Dallas Cowboys
1978	Archie Manning, New Orleans Saints
1977	Lyle Alzado, Denver Broncos
1976	Jim Hart, St. Louis Cardinals
1975	Rocky Bleier, Pittsburgh Steelers
1974	Floyd Little, Denver Broncos
1973	Andy Russell, Pittsburgh Steelers
1972	Ray May, Baltimore Colts
1971	Kermit Alexander, Los Angeles Rams
1970	Gale Sayers, Chicago Bears
1969	Ed Meador, Los Angeles Rams
1968	Willie Davis, Green Bay Packers
1967	Bart Starr, Green Bay Packers

Walter Payton NFL
Man of the Year Award Winners

2007	Jason Taylor, defensive end, Miami Dolphins
2006	Drew Brees, quarterback, New Orleans Saints and LaDainian Tomlinson, running back, San Diego
2005	Peyton Manning, quarterback, Indianapolis Colts
2004	Warrick Dunn, running back, Atlanta Falcons
2003	Will Shields, guard, Kansas City Chiefs
2002	Troy Vincent, cornerback, Philadelphia Eagles
2001	Jerome Bettis, running back, Pittsburgh Steelers
2000	Derrick Brooks, linebacker, Tampa Bay Buccaneers and Jim Flanigan, defensive end, Chicago Bears
1999	Cris Carter, wide receiver, Minnesota Vikings
1998	Dan Marino, quarterback, Miami Dolphins
1997	Troy Aikman, quarterback, Dallas Cowboys
1996	Darrell Green, cornerback, Washington Redskins
1995	Boomer Esiason, quarterback, New York Jets
1994	Junior Seau, linebacker, San Diego Chargers
1993	Derrick Thomas, linebacker, Kansas City Chiefs
1992	John Elway, quarterback, Denver Broncos
1991	Anthony Muñoz, tackle, Cincinnati Bengals
1990	Mike Singletary, linebacker, Chicago Bears
1989	Warren Moon, quarterback, Houston Oilers
1988	Steve Largent, wide receiver, Seattle Seahawks
1987	Dave Duerson, safety, Chicago Bears
1986	Reggie Williams, linebacker, Cincinnati Bengals
1985	Dwight Stephenson, center, Miami Dolphins
1984	Marty Lyons, defensive tackle, New York Jets
1983	Rolf Benirschke, kicker, San Diego Chargers
1982	Joe Theismann, quarterback, Washington Redskins
1981	Lynn Swann, wide receiver, Pittsburgh Steelers
1980	Harold Carmichael, wide receiver, Philadelphia Eagles
1979	Joe Greene, defensive lineman, Pittsburgh Steelers
1978	Roger Staubach, quarterback, Dallas Cowboys
1977	Walter Payton, running back, Chicago Bears
1976	Franco Harris, running back, Pittsburgh Steelers
1975	Ken Anderson, quarterback, Cincinnati Bengals
1974	George Blanda, quarterback, Oakland Raiders
1973	Len Dawson, quarterback, Kansas City Chiefs
1972	Willie Lanier, linebacker, Kansas City Chiefs
1971	John Hadl, quarterback, San Diego Chargers
1970	Johnny Unitas, quarterback, Baltimore Colts

Bart Starr Award Winners

2008	LaDainian Tomlinson, San Diego Chargers
2007	John Lynch, Denver Broncos
2006	Curtis Martin, New York Jets
2005	Troy Vincent, Buffalo Bills
2004	Derrick Brooks, Tampa Bay Buccaneers
2003	Trent Dilfer, Seattle Seahawks
2002	Darren Woodson, Dallas Cowboys
2001	Bruce Matthews, Tennessee Titans
2000	Aeneas Williams, Arizona Cardinals
1999	Eugene Robinson, Atlanta Falcons
1998	Irving Fryar, Philadelphia Eagles and Brent Jones, San Francisco 49ers
1997	Darrell Green, Washington Redskins
1996	Jackie Slater, St. Louis Rams
1995	Cris Carter, Minnesota Vikings
1994	Warren Moon, Houston Oilers
1993	Gill Byrd, San Diego Chargers
1992	Reggie White, Philadelphia Eagles
1991	Mike Singletary, Chicago Bears
1990	Anthony Muñoz, Cincinnati Bengals
1989	Steve Largent, Seattle Seahawks

RESOURCES

Part One: **George Martin:** *The Transcontinental Traverse*

Anderson, Dave. "Sports of The Times: A Long Walk for Those Who Responded to 9/11." www.sportingnews.com/blog/metsfan62/93673 - 63k, July 12, 2007.

Betton, Kim. "Retired NY Giants Great George Martin Honored in Little Rock on 'A Journey for 9/11' Charitable Walk Across U.S." KARK 4 News.http://arkansasmatters.com/content/fulltext/?cid=63979, Jan 8, 2008.

Donnelly, Mike. "News: George Martin - A Journey For 9/11." NFLPlayers.com. http://www.nflplayers.com/news/news_release.aspx?id=7239, 09/12/2007.

Carroll, Bob and Michael Gershman, David Neft, John Thorn, et al. *Total Football II: The Official Encyclopedia of the National Football League.* New York City: HarperCollins*Publishers*, 1999.

Diaz, George. Personal interview. 20 Nov. 2007.

Eisen, Michael. "George Martin Walks for the First Responders of 9/11." *Touchdown: The Official Newsletter of the New York Giants, 2007 Season Kickoff Issue.* East Rutherford, New Jersey: 6, 8.

Hanlon, Pat and Ed Croke. *1993 Giants Official Information Guide.* New York City: New York Giants, 1993.

Kernan, Kevin. "Giant Steps: On the Road with George Martin on his Journey for 9/11." *New York Post.* http://www.nypost.com/seven/11182007/sports/giants/giant_steps_407600.htm?page=0, Nov. 18, 2007.

King, Peter. "Monday Morning Quarterback: A Giant cause: Martin walks for Ground Zero victims; Fine 15, more." SI.com. http://sportsillustrated.cnn.com /2007/writers/peter_king/12/16/week15/index.html, Dec. 17, 2007.

Leaser, Michael. "Gridiron Giving: The National Football League's All-Star Philanthropists. Philanthropy Magazine. http://www.philanthropyroundtable.org /article.asp?article=1513&cat=147, Feb. 20, 2008.

Martin, Dianne. Personal interview. 20 Nov. 2007.

Martin, George. Personal interviews. 20 Nov. 2007, 11 March 2008.

Mcshane, Larry. "Ex-NFL star George Martin starts walk to raise $10 million for 9/11 rescue workers." *USA Today* (Associated Press). http://www.usatoday.com /sports/football/2007-09-15-3572942149_x.htm, Feb. 16, 2008.

Messick, Dave. Personal interview. 20 Nov. 2007.

Messick, John. Personal interview. 20 Nov. 2007.

Minoch, Patra. Personal interview. 20 Nov. 2007.

Murphey, Kerry. "The Final Lap: Celebs make their Daytona 500 picks." http://www.finallapradio.com/content/view/768/45/, Feb. 14, 2008.

NFLDraftBible.com. "Heisman Trophy Trust to Honor Retired NY Giants Great George Martin on December 10." http://nfldraftbible.blogspot.com/search /label/GEORGE%20MARTIN, Dec. 8, 2007.

NYDailyNews.com. "Ex-Giant calls timeout on 9/11 walk." http://www.nydaily news.com/sports/football/giants/2008/01/23/2008-01-23_exgiant_calls _timeout_on_911_walk.html, January 23rd 2008.

Pro-football-reference.com.

Reeves, Lee. Personal interviews. 20 Nov. 2007, 11 March 2008, 12 March 2008.

Rhoden, William C. "Sports Of The Times: Miles to Go Before Martin Finishes Journey." NYTimes.com. http://www.nytimes.com/2008/01/31/sports /football/31rhoden.html, Jan. 31, 2008.

Wikipedia, the free encyclopedia. "George Martin (American football)." http://en.wikipedia.org/wiki/George_Martin_(American_football).

Part Two: Tony Dungy: *Staying the Course*

Associated Press. "More than 2,000 help Dungy bury his son: Colts coach doesn't say when he will return; Bush sends condolences." Msnbc.com. http://www.msnbc.msn.com/id/10588799/, Dec. 28, 2005.

Blaising, Steve. Personal interview. 18 Jan. 2008.

Brown, Abe. Personal interview. 25 May 2007.

Brown, Clifton. "Jones Faces Felony Charges in Las Vegas." NYTimes.com. http://www.nytimes.com/2007/06/21/sports/football/21nfl.html, June 21, 2007.

Carroll, Bob and Michael Gershman, David Neft, John Thorn, et al. *Total Football*

II: The Official Encyclopedia of the National Football League. New York City: HarperCollins*Publishers*, 1999.

Dungy, Tony. Personal interview. 23 May 2007.

Dungy, Tony with Nathan Whitaker. *Quiet Strength: The Principles, Practices, & Priorities of a Winning Life.* Carol Stream, Ill.: Tyndale House Publishers Inc., 2007.

d9a2v4. Yahoo! Sports "NFL Rumors." http://sports.yahoo.com/nfl/rumors /post/Bucs-players-put-on-notice?urn=nfl,16801&cp=4, Dec 5, 2006.

Fitzgerald, Pat. Personal interview. 21 Jan. 2008.

Gray, Darrin. Personal interview. 15 Jan. 2008.

Patrick, Dan. "Just My Type: The Fine Print." *Sports Illustrated.* 24 March 2008: 36.

Pro-football-reference.com.

Saturday, Jeff. Personal interview. 5 June 2007.

Wikipedia, the free encyclopedia. "Chris Henry (wide receiver): Criminal history." http://en.wikipedia.org/wiki/Chris_Henry_(wide_receiver).

Part Three: **Warrick Dunn**: *Noble Enabler*

Arena, Rita. Personal interviews. 13, 15 Nov. 2007.

Boe, Natalie. Personal interview. 13 Nov. 2007.

Chadiha, Jeffri. Inside the NFL: "Carrying a load: Therapy helps Warrick Dunn put the pieces together." SI.com. http://sportsillustrated.cnn.com/2005 /writers/jeffri_chadiha/04/05/dunn.therapy/index.html, April 5, 2005.

Carroll, Bob and Michael Gershman, David Neft, John Thorn, et al. *Total Football II: The Official Encyclopedia of the National Football League.* New York City: HarperCollinsPublishers, 1999.

Dungy, Tony with Nathan Whitaker. *Quiet Strength: The Principles, Practices, and Priorities of a Winning Life.* Carol Stream, Ill.: Tyndale House Publishers, 2007.

Dunn, Warrick. Personal interview. 13 Nov. 2007.

Fanning, Joele. Personal interview. 13 Nov. 2007.

Forbes.com. "Atlanta Falcons' Warrick Dunn Wins Inaugural The Home Depot NFL Neighborhood MVP Award." http://www.forbes.com/prnewswire/feeds /prnewswire/2008/01/30/prnewswire200801301430PR_NEWS_USPR _CLW092.html, Jan. 30, 2008.

Keith, Melanie. Personal interviews. 13, 16 Nov. 2007.

Keith, Otis. Personal interview. 13 Nov. 2007.

Krix, Jennifer. Personal interview. 13 Nov. 2007.

kwchamber. "Day 28 - Part 2." Protrade.com. http://www.protrade.com /content/DisplayArticle.html?sp=S94cd3e9e-40fb-11dc-808f-4188e562aa5b, Aug. 2, 2007.

Leaser, Michael. "Gridiron Giving: The National Football League's All-Star Philanthropists. Philanthropy Magazine. http://www.philanthropyroundtable.org
/article.asp?article=1513&cat=147, Feb. 20, 2008.

Miles, Billy. Personal interview. 13 Nov. 2007.

Miles, Tiffany. Personal interviews. 13, 15 Nov. 2007.

Nasiri, Rona. Personal interview. 13 Nov. 2007.

Newsiasm: Beyond-the-Headlines, Positively Inspired News: "Warrick Dunn;
Beyond the Field to Help Single Mothers." http://209.85.207.104
/search?q=cache:6Sx7UESsGDkJ:newsiasm.com/beyond-the-headlines/
Children/315/warrick_dunn_beyond_the_field_to_help_single_mothers+%22
NFL+Star+and+Philanthropist+Warrick+Dunn%22&hl=en&ct=clnk&cd=1&gl
=us, April 17, 2007.

NFLPlayers.com. "Players: Warrick Dunn, #28." http://www.nflplayers.com
/players/player.aspx?id=25097.

NFL Players.com. "Warrick Dunn #28." http://www.nflplayers.com/players
/player.aspx?id=25097.

Pro-football-reference.com.

Sanders, Shannon. Personal interviews. 13, 16 Nov. 2007.

Savage, Kia. Personal interviews. 13, 16 Nov. 2007.

Stubbings, Beth. Personal interview. 13 Nov. 2007.

Williams, Jacquelyn. Personal interviews. 13, 15 Nov. 2007.

Part Four: **They Also Serve**

Atlantafalcons.com. "Keith Brooking, LB #56." http://www.atlantafalcons.com
/People/Players/Active/Keith_Brooking.aspx.

Attner, Paul. "Good Guys: Rushing to Katrina aid." SportingNews.com.
http://www.sportingnews.com/exclusives/20060623/750711-p.html, June
23, 2006.

Azcardinals.com. "Community Pages: Foundations." http://www.azcardinals.com
/community/foundations.php.

Campus Crusade for Christ. "LaDainian Tomlinson Receives Bart Starr Award."
http://www.ccci.org/ministries/athletes-in-action/ladainian-tomlinson-bart-
starr-award.aspx, Feb. 2, 2008.

Carroll, Bob and Michael Gershman, David Neft, John Thorn, et al. *Total Football
II: The Official Encyclopedia of the National Football League.* New York City:
HarperCollinsPublishers, 1999.

Chicagobears.com. "Roster: 14, Brian Griese." http://www.chicagobears.com
/team/player31.html, 2007.

Denverbroncos.com. "47 John Lynch, Safety." http://www.denverbroncos.com
/page.php?id=498&contentID=2240.

Derrick Brooks Charities Official Web Site. "Derrick Brooks Bio."
http://www.derrickbrookscharities.org/.

Donalddriverfoundation.com. http://www.donalddriverfoundation.com/flash
/index.html.

Fennelly, Martin. Orig. *The Tampa Tribune*, "Dilfer Turns A Tragedy Into Inspiration." http://www.bucpower.com/feature-dilfer.html, 21 September 2004.

Houstontexans.com. "Player Outreach: Kris Brown's Kick Club."
http://www.houstontexans.com/community/Outreach.asp.

Hyde, Dave. "Dolphins' Taylor making a real impact off the field." South Florida
Sun-Sentinel.com. http://jasontaylorfoundation.com/PDFs/Dave%20Hyde
%201-20-08.pdf, Jan. 20, 2008.

Johnlynchfoundation.com. http://www.johnlynchfoundation.com/default.asp.

Johnson, Derrick. "Lead by example: Kansas City Chiefs linebacker Derrick Johnson inspires kids to excel." http://www.usaweekend.com/07_issues/071007
/071007diffday-nfl-gives.html. Oct. 7, 2007.

Kidsclub.buccaneers.com. "He's the Man." http://kidsclub.buccaneers.com/news
/newsprint.aspx?newsid=2756.

Krisbrownskickclub.com http://www.krisbrownskickclub.com.

Kurtwarner.org.

Madariaga, Katherine. "Clements Named 49ers Walter Payton Man of the Year."
http://49ers.com/pressbox/news_detail.php?PRKey=3852&section
=PR%20News, Dec. 19, 2007.

Miamidolphins.com. "Dolphins DE Jason Taylor Named Walter Payton NFL
Man of the Year." http://www.miamidolphins.com/newsite/news/top_story
_print.asp?contentID=5666, Feb. 3, 2008.

National Football League Players Association. "Charity Work: NFL Players Gala
featuring the JB Awards." http://www.nflpa.org/CharityWork/GridironGala.aspx.

Neworleanssaints.com. "NFL Player Page: Drew Brees, QB."
http://www.neworleanssaints.com/Team/Roster/People/Drew%20Brees.aspx.

Peyton Manning official web site: News Room. "Colts Quarterback Peyton Manning Named Walter Payton NFL Man of the Year." http://pm.web-pros.com
/newsroom/newsreleases/020306.cfm, February 3, 2006.

Pro-football-reference.com.

SBS—The Business of the NFL. "QB Trent Dilfer Comes Home To San Francisco - *Oakland Tribune*." http://nflbiz.blogspot.com/2006/05/qb-trent-
dilfer-comes-home-to-san.html, May 22, 2006.

Sf49ers.com. "Trent Dilfer, #12." http://www.sf49ers.com/team/roster_
detail.php?PRKey=80&section=TE+Roster.

Simon, Bob. "L.T.: Off-Field Work Is More Important." CBS News.com: *60
Minutes*. http://www.cbsnews.com/stories/2007/12/06/60minutes/main
3585567.shtml, Dec. 9, 2007.

Texas Children's Hospital. "Get Involved: Special events: Kris Brown's Kick Club."
http://www.texaschildrens.org/waystogive/FinancialSupport/KBKC.aspx.

thigh master. "Darrell Green's Super Bowl Blog: 28 at XLII."
http://blog.washingtonpost.com/darrellgreen/2008/01/redskins_coaching_
search.html, Jan. 30, 2008.

TIME.com. "Hurricane Katrina – Two Years later: Katrina Anniversary, Deuce
McAllister." http://www.time.com/time/specials/2007/article/0,28804,
1646611_1646683_1647809,00.html.

Titansonline.com. "Bulluck named Community Man of the Year for 2007."
http://www.titansonline.com/news/newsmain_detail.php?PRKey=5388,
Dec. 3, 2007.

Varley, Teresa. "Ward a finalist for Walter Payton Man of the Year." Steelers.com.
http://news.steelers.com/article/86959/.

Wikipedia, the free encyclopedia. "Athletes in Action/Bart Starr Award."
http://en.wikipedia.org/wiki/Bart_Starr_Award.

Wikipedia, the free encyclopedia. "Brian Griese." http://en.wikipedia.org/wiki
/Brian_Griese.

Wikipedia, the free encyclopedia. "Derrick Brooks." http://en.wikipedia.org
/wiki/Derrick_Brooks.

Wikipedia, the free encyclopedia. "Grant Wistrom." http://en.wikipedia.org
/wiki/Grant_Wistrom.

WunschFamilyFoundation.org. http://www.wunschfamilyfoundation.org
/index.html.

Index

251